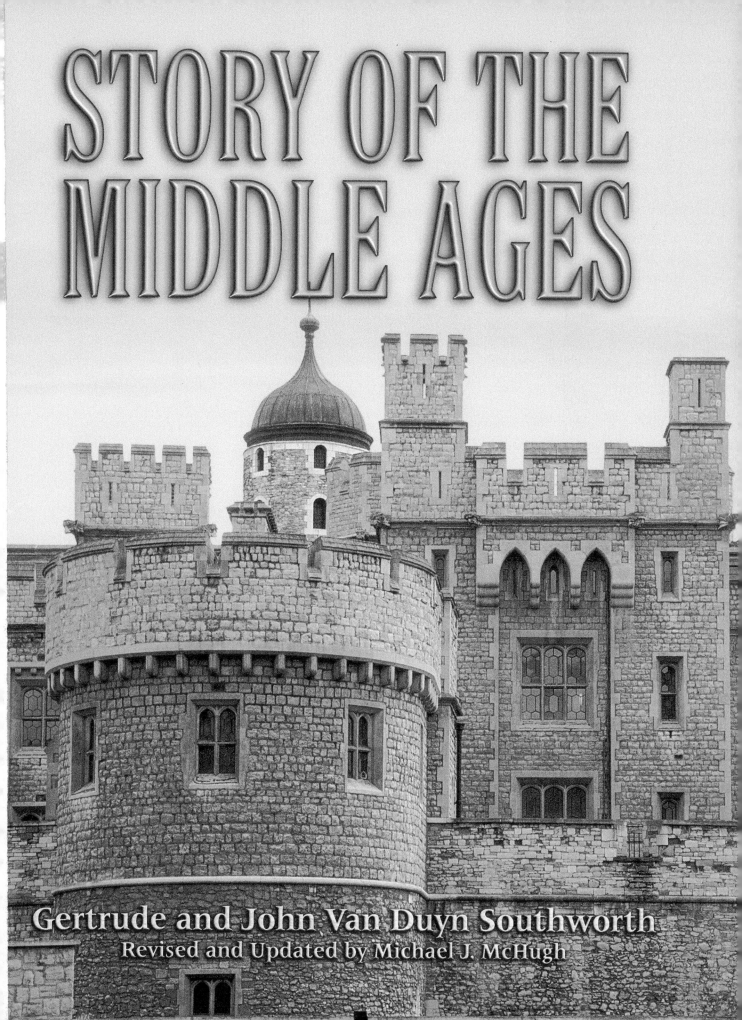

STORY OF THE MIDDLE AGES

Gertrude and John Van Duyn Southworth
Revised and Updated by Michael J. McHugh

ORIGINALLY ENTITLED: *The Story of the Middle Ages*
ORIGINALLY PUBLISHED BY: Iroquois Publishing Company, Inc. Syracuse, NY © 1934

A publication of
Christian Liberty Press

502 West Euclid Avenue
Arlington Heights, Illinois 60004
www.christianlibertypress.com

Scripture references are conformed to The Holy Bible, New King James Version © 1982, Thomas Nelson, Inc., so that modern readers may gain greater comprehension of the Word of God.

Written by Gertrude and John Van Duyn Southworth
Revised and updated by Michael J. McHugh
Edited by Edward J. Shewan
Layout and design by Bob Fine

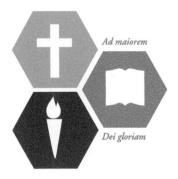

Ad maiorem

Dei gloriam

CHRISTIAN LIBERTY PRESS
502 West Euclid Avenue
Arlington Heights, Illinois 60004
www.christianlibertypress.com   ISBN 1-930367-77-7

Image Credits: Grateful acknowledgement is given to Dover Publications for use of their copyright images which appear on pages 3, 9, 12, 13, 15, 24, 42, 46, 48, 53, 56, 72, 79, 99.

Printed in the United States of America

Contents

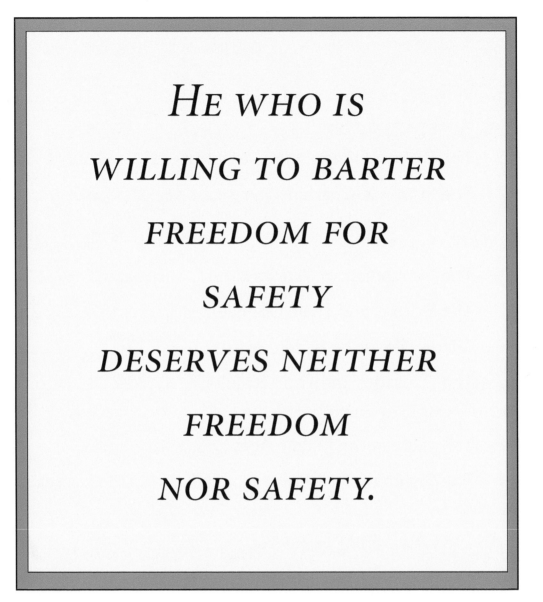

He who is willing to barter freedom for safety deserves neither freedom nor safety.

INTRODUCTION

HISTORY REVOLVES AROUND CHRIST

D id you ever wonder why historians often divide history according to the time before Christ (B.C.) and the period after He was born (A.D.—*anno Domini*, which means "in the year of the Lord")? It is because all of world history revolves around or centers upon the work of Christ in history. No other person in all of human history compares to Jesus Christ. The fact that Jesus Christ is the author of history and has changed the course of world events more than any other person, qualifies Him for the distinction of being at the center of world history. This is in spite of the fact that He was born in poverty and lived a very short and simple existence on Earth. A truly wise student of history is one who recognizes the preeminent status of Christ. Every event from Creation to Calvary pointed toward the work of the Lord Jesus Christ, every event after Christ's resurrection looks forward to His return as the conquering King of kings.

Christ alone is King of kings and Lord of lords

Christians joyfully acknowledge the fact that the Son of God, Jesus Christ, was able to have a miraculous impact upon world history, because of His dual nature as Almighty God and sinless man; and yet secular historians have also marveled at what Christ accomplished in His humanity. It is noteworthy that the unbelieving world is commonly willing to give a certain degree of recognition to the accomplishments of Christ because He was such an extraordinary figure. Consider for a few moments the following facts concerning the Christ of history:

Jesus was a man conceived of the Holy Spirit, born in an obscure village, the child of a Jewish peasant woman. He grew up in another obscure village. He worked in a carpenter shop until he was thirty, and then for three years was an itinerant preacher. He never wrote a book. He never held political office. He never had a family. He never went to college. He seldom put his foot inside a big city. He never traveled 200 miles from the place where He was born. He never did one of the things that the world would call great. While He was still a young man, the tide of popular opinion turned against Him. His friends ran away. He was turned over to His enemies. He went through a trial that was a mockery of justice.

His executioners gambled for the only piece of property He had—His coat. After Christ was unjustly executed, He was taken down and laid in a borrowed grave through the pity of a friend. After three days, He arose from the dead, but because He did not appear before unbelievers, His resurrection and ascension were never recognized. Twenty wide centuries have come and gone, and today, He is the Centerpiece of much of the human race. All the armies that have ever marched, ... all the navies that ever were built, ... all the parliaments that ever sat, ... all the kings that ever reigned ... PUT TOGETHER ... have not affected the life of man upon this earth as powerfully as has that ... ONE SOLITARY LIFE.

As we begin to study the events of history that unfolded after the earthly ministry of Christ, we must be sure to give Him proper acknowledgment as the King of kings and Lord of lords. As Paul the Apostle told the leaders at Athens, in the first century after Christ, "God, who made the world and everything in it, since He is Lord of heaven and earth, does not dwell in temples made with hands. Nor is He worshiped with men's hands, as though He needed anything, since He gives to all life, breath, and all things. And He has made from one blood every nation of men to dwell on all the face of the earth, and has determined their preappointed times and the boundaries of their dwellings…" (Acts 17:24–26).

When we study history, we study the effects of God's eternal purposes upon people and nations. From the beginning of time, the Triune God has been at work to ordain and to accomplish His purposes through every event that happens. The Lord created all the different nationalities of people—Americans, Australians, Chinese, Egyptians, Germans, Brazilians, and more. It is God's perfect will and sovereign power that causes nations to rise and fall. The Lord raises up kings and humbles princes, for all power belongs to God and He loans a portion of His power to those of His choosing for a season.

It is the Lord, therefore, who chooses where on Earth each nation should be located and which boundaries—rivers, mountains, oceans—that should fence them in. As many writers have noted, all of history is actually "His Story." The wisdom of Almighty God in planning each and every detail of history to accomplish His purposes is truly incredible. All praise and honor belong to the powerful God of Scripture who causes everything to happen just as He has planned for His own glory.

No student of history should ever be foolish enough to think that the story of world history is simply a record of man's accomplishments and failures over the ages. True history is preoccupied with analyzing world events in the light of God's plan to redeem a community of believers unto Himself out of every nation and tribe through the Gospel of Christ. For this reason, the progress of the church—which is made up of believers from every nation—should be of paramount interest to historians. Sadly, however, students of history often refuse to acknowledge God's providential control over world events. In the end, such secular historians rob themselves of the privilege of glorying in the acts of the Almighty Creator by choosing to focus upon the acts of sinful creatures alone.

THE MIDDLE AGES

The Middle Ages was an important period in world history, because it prepared the way for (1) the great spiritual awakening, known as the Reformation, and (2) the spread of the Gospel during the Age of Exploration. The Middle Ages received its name due to the fact that this time period takes place between ancient and modern times. The time we call the Middle Ages began in A.D. 476, the year when the Germanic tribes overthrew the last emperor of the Western Roman Empire. It ended more than a thousand years later, about 1500. This was shortly after the voyages of Columbus to the Americas. The first part of the Middle Ages, from A.D. 476 until about the year A.D. 1000, is known as the Dark Ages, because during this time many people in Western Europe were ignorant, poor, and miserable. Not long after the Dark Ages, during a transitional period within the Middle Ages, the Crusades began. For almost two hundred years, from A.D. 1096 until A.D. 1291, the people of Western Europe sent army after army into southwestern Asia to try to take the Holy Land of Palestine and keep it under Christian control. The last part of the Middle Ages is known as the Renaissance, or High Middle Ages. This was a time when the people of Western Europe began to take an interest in art and learning and to make discoveries and inventions. The Renaissance lasted from about A.D. 1300 until about A.D. 1500.

THE REFORMATION

The Renaissance closed as the great Protestant Reformation era began. This era lasted from A.D. 1517, when Luther wrote his *Ninety-five Theses*, until A.D. 1648, when the Westminster Confession of Faith was adopted by England and Scotland. During the High Middle Ages, God began to move in the hearts of men such as John Wycliffe, in England, and John Huss, in Bohemia. These and many others began to criticize the doctrines and government of the Roman Catholic Church. Wealth and power had so corrupted the Church that radical reform was necessary. "In the fullness of time" the Reformation came into full bloom, when the conditions were ripe. God used such men as Martin Luther and John Calvin to bring about this radical reform, which spread throughout Europe and even to the British colonies in North America. During this era, many Confessions of Faith and catechisms—delineating the truths of Scripture—were written, such as Luther's *Shorter Catechism*, Calvin's *Catechism*, the *Gallic Confession* (France), the *Belgic Confession* (The Netherlands), the *Heidelberg Catechism* (Germany), the *Thirty-nine Articles* (England), and the *Westminster Confession of Faith*—including the *Larger* and *Shorter Catechisms*.

THE AGE OF EXPLORATION

The Middle Ages was followed by the Age of Exploration, which lasted from about 1492 until 1682. During this period of time, daring explorers from Europe crossed sea and land to discover unknown parts of the New World and claim them as possessions of the countries under whose flags they sailed. During this time, many explorers and missionaries also took the Gospel to many parts of the known world.

The following timeline shows the various periods of history, which will be covered in this book. Carefully examine this timeline. You will find it helpful to refer back to it as you study about the Middle Ages.

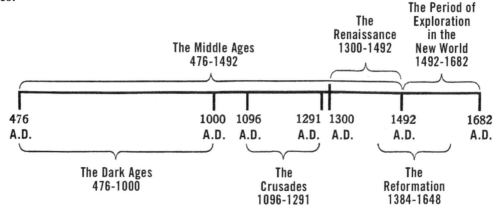

Chapter 1
WHY STUDY ABOUT THE MIDDLE AGES?

WHERE DID AMERICANS COME FROM?

Are there any boys and girls reading this book who were not born in America? How many of you have parents who were born in some other country? Many of us have grandparents and great-grandparents who are natives of the United States, but few of us can trace our family histories back for more than two or three hundred years without finding that our ancestors came to America from other lands.

There are more than two hundred and eighty million of us now, but many of us are the descendants of immigrants who came to the New World from beyond the Atlantic or Pacific Oceans. Many of us look back to the pleasant fields of England, to the hills of Scotland, or to the green shores of Ireland as "Our Old Home." In addition to these English-speaking people, the citizens of every land in Europe have come to help make our country—especially Germany, Italy, France, the Netherlands, and Switzerland. Others hail from Scandinavia—Sweden, Norway, and Denmark. While most of our people came from European ancestors, about thirty million of them, who have dark skin, are descended from Negro slaves who were brought against their wills from the continent of Africa. It is loyalty to our Constitution and to our ideals, however, that makes people who come to the United States good citizens, whether they hail from Africa, Asia, Australia, Europe, or Latin America.

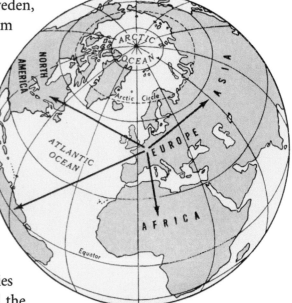

The continent of Europe was on center stage during the Middle Ages.

In many cases our family names suggest the countries from which our people came. The Browns and the Clarks, the Robinsons and the Taylors, as well as the Binghams and the Washingtons and all other families whose names end in "ham" or "ton" are from England. The Mackenzies and the Buchanans are of Scottish descent. The Kellys and the O'Connors once called Ireland their home. The first Petersons and Carlsons came from Sweden. The Schmidts hail from Germany, the Lamonts from France, and the Giovannis from Italy. The Garcias came from Mexico, the Romanovs from Russia, the Wongs from China, the Patels from India, and the Wah'abis from Egypt. But whatever our names or the lands of our ancestors, if we love liberty and godly virtue we are true Americans.

Where there is much heavy work to be done, as in the coal mines of West Virginia, the steel mills of Gary, Indiana, or the building of skyscrapers in Chicago, we find many newcomers from other places around the world. Many recent immigrants are building and repairing our transportation system, working in our mills and factories, and helping grow our economy in every way. Loyal newcomers and their children, as much as those whose ancestors have been long in the land, are the Americans of the future. All loyal citizens can say, "This is our country."

Why Europeans Came to America

It is more than four hundred years since the first Europeans began to establish permanent settlements in the country we now call America. From the beginning, those who came have been writing back to their relatives and friends about the opportunities in their new homes. In this way, the few who came first have been enticing larger and larger numbers every year to come to America, the land of promise. The number of immigrants has often varied over the years up to the present time. Recently, however, as many as a million new immigrants have landed on our shores in a single year, and many of these newcomers came from Asia and Latin America, not from Europe. For a long time everyone who came was welcomed. Now we have laws shutting out paupers, criminals, and those who have dangerous diseases.

Nearly all the people who have come to America—from the nation's earliest history to the present time—came because they wanted to be free, or because they wanted a better chance to make a living than the Old World could give them. Some of them fled from the tyranny of oppressive governments, others came to win the right to worship God in their own way, while many were driven out by the poverty in the overcrowded lands of their old homes. America has been the land of liberty and of opportunity to one and all from the earliest to the latest comer.

This is a red-letter day for these immigrants. In becoming naturalized citizens, they agree to "support and defend the Constitution and laws of the United States against all enemies."

How Our Ancestors Crossed the Atlantic

Many millions of immigrants have come to America in large ocean liners. Their voyage lasted only a few days and was made without great hardship. It was not so with the earlier settlers who came to our country. Their passage across the Atlantic was a long and dangerous one, sometimes lasting many weeks. It was made in small sailing vessels where the passengers often suffered greatly because of crowded quarters and poor food. Disease frequently broke out on shipboard and many died. In one example, about three hundred years ago a shipload of one hundred and fifty settlers started out for America. One hundred of them died on the voyage. A little later there was another ship in which, out of the four hundred who sailed, only one hundred and five lived to reach America.

In many cases, only the strong were able to survive the awful hardships of the old-time voyage from Europe to America. Of those who reached the new land, only the most courageous could long withstand the exposure, the diseases, and the Indian fighting which they faced as they cleared the land and built their new homes in the wilderness. The hardy and vigorous men and women who lived through the trying experience of those early days were the ancestors of many Americans today. We may well sing of our country as— "The land of the free and the home of the brave."

What Americans Brought from the Old World

The Europeans who came to be Americans were civilized people. They brought their manners, their customs, and their ideals with them. They planted the civilization of their homelands in America. Our American life and civilization have grown from what was planted by our forefathers.

Civilization is a long, hard word, but we shall not find it difficult to understand what it means. By civilized people, we mean people who have laws that reflect a knowledge of God and a government that enforces obedience to these laws. They are people who cultivate the soil; who carry on commerce; who own property, houses, cars, and businesses; who attend schools, churches, and civic events; who enjoy books, art, and music. In a word, people who live very much as we do now.

The settlers in America often brought with them, from their past experiences in Europe, the knowledge of how God's law and the Christian faith could help them live a good life. They brought with them, therefore, many ideas and biblical beliefs about right and wrong and about their duties to God and to other men. These ideas and beliefs were at the foundation of their civilization or culture.

The noble ways of doing things and the time-honored ideals of hard work, self-sacrifice and the Golden Rule which make up what we call civilization, have recently come under attack in America, yet some of them have been wonderfully developed. The origin of our Western civilization flows primarily from the spring of a European culture that was shaped by Christianity in general, and the sixteenth-century Protestant Reformation in particular. It is important, therefore, that all students gain an understanding of the influence of European civilization upon the formation of the United States.

It had taken men thousands of years to learn what they knew when they first began to come from Europe to America hundreds of years ago. The story of the way civilized ideas of living grew up in the Old World is as much a part of our history as the story of the way the European peoples first brought these ideas to the shores of America. This book will permit students to read about both of these stories.

CHAPTER SUMMARY

Most of the early immigrants to the United States came from the continent of Europe. For this reason, many of the cultural traditions, legal standards, and religious beliefs of the United States reflect the values that were held by the people who lived in Europe centuries ago.

Many European immigrants came to the United States to escape the tyranny of wicked rulers and to enjoy the ability to worship God freely. Other immigrants came to the Americas to find better jobs and economic opportunity.

During the twentieth century, millions of new immigrants began to enter the United States from non-European nations. In recent years, most of the immigrants have come from Latin America and Asia. These newer citizens were able to travel to the United States by swift airplanes or comfortable ocean liners. In the early days of American history, the people who came to the United States often suffered great hardships coming to our shores.

The foundation of American culture sprang from a European society that was greatly influenced by biblical Christianity in general, and the sixteenth-century Protestant Reformation in particular. Most of the laws and social traditions of early American society clearly reflected the dynamic influence of Christianity upon this period of history. ∎

CHAPTER QUESTIONS AND ACTIVITIES

1. Locate on a map of Europe all the countries named in this chapter.
2. What is your own mother country?
3. Why did your ancestors come to America?
4. Find out all you can about how your ancestors lived in their Old World homes.
5. Talk with a recent immigrant about his journey to America.
6. Ask a recent immigrant how America differs from his homeland.
7. Should the U.S. government further restrict immigration? If so, why?
8. What can we do to help the newcomers in our country to become virtuous Americans?
9. What was the primary "spring" that shaped the flow of Western civilization?

KEY TERMS

Immigrant   Culture
Civilization   Society
Protestant   Citizen

Chapter 2
THE ROMAN EMPIRE AND CHRISTIANITY

More than two thousand years ago (27 B.C.), the people of Rome conquered much of the known world and brought it under their rule. All problems which arose in the different countries that Rome had conquered were settled by their Roman governors or by the Roman emperor himself. The Roman armies did any fighting which had to be done. More and more, the people of the conquered countries came to depend on Rome for almost everything. For more than four hundred years, the Romans held their great empire together. Then Rome lost her power and many of the countries she had ruled were left without governments and without protection.

The Roman Empire dominated the ancient world prior to the opening of the Middle Ages.

The Roman Empire

Halfway down the western slope of the Central Apennines Mountains in Italy stands a group of seven hills. On these hills, more than twenty-seven hundred years ago, the city of Rome was founded.

From the earliest days, the Romans were great fighters. They captured neighboring towns one by one until, in time, they ruled all of Italy. Still they were not satisfied. Their armies on land, and their ships upon the sea, conquered nation after nation. Western and Southern Europe, as well as many countries of Asia and Africa, came under Roman rule. The taxes that these conquered peoples paid made the Roman nation the richest in the world.

The men who ruled the mighty Roman Empire were called emperors. The greatest of these was Caesar Augustus, who became emperor in 27 B.C.—about twenty-three years before the birth of Christ. Because Augustus brought peace and prosperity to Rome, his reign was spoken of as the Golden Age, or *Pax Romana*. During the rule of Augustus and the emperors who followed him in the next one hundred and fifty years, Rome became a very beautiful city, and the empire reached the height of its power. In the early stages of the government of Rome, it functioned as a republic where much of the ruling power was vested in a body of men known as senators. The Roman Senate, which represented the people, was most active prior to the establishment of the vast Roman Empire with its powerful emperors.

At its height, Roman civilization had a highly developed culture with comprehensive laws and a refined social order.

As time went on, however, Rome became increasingly corrupt and immoral and began to lose her hold over the lands she ruled. In the early days of Rome, the people had worked together for the good of Rome. Now, however, the rich and immoral ruling class had gained control of most of the land and the poor farmers had no way to support themselves. Thousands of them flocked to the cities in search of work, but there was not enough work for them because the majority of business owners used slave labor. To prevent trouble, the government had to supply the unemployed mob with food and entertainment to prevent rioting. These problems also forced the Roman government to raise taxes on those who could find work and the heavy taxes eventually caused such citizens to revolt.

Roman society was filled with slaves from conquered territories. On occasion, some of these slaves would unite and revolt against their Roman masters. These revolts would often end badly for the slaves as they would be captured and executed by way of crucifixion. Roman justice was quick and cruel, but the horrible death of crucifixion was normally reserved for the worst of criminals.

The Roman armies, which had been so strong, were by A.D. 250 largely made up of men from the conquered countries, which did not love Rome as the Romans had. Finally, in the year A.D. 395, which means three hundred and ninety-five years after the birth of Christ, the Roman emperor died, leaving the empire to his two sons to divide it between themselves. Rome became the capital of the Western Roman Empire and Constantinople the capital of the Eastern Roman Empire. This division of the empire weakened the power of the Romans still more as various rulers fought with each other over land disputes.

The city of Rome was overrun by barbarian tribes in A.D. 410 and the Western Roman Empire eventually collapsed in A.D. 476.

Heavy taxes and immoral laws caused the Roman Empire's fall.

The Life and Teachings of Jesus

In the days of the first Roman emperor, Caeser Augustus, Jesus was born in Judea. At that time, Judea was a part of the Roman Empire, and the Roman governors treated the Jews cruelly. The Jews yearned for political freedom, and looked for a deliverer. When Jesus became a teacher and leader of His people, His lofty principles, moral courage, and miraculous power convinced His disciples and followers that He was the one that was ordained to deliver them from the yoke of Rome. Sadly, these people did not understand the true mission of the Son of God, who was sent to set elect sinners free from the bondage of their sins and provide them with eternal life.

Shortly before His crucifixion, the Messiah Jesus made a processional entry into Jerusalem, the chief city of the Roman province of Judea, with great crowds shouting loudly and proclaiming Him, "King of the Jews." This proclamation was eventually used by a group of powerful and influential Jewish religious leaders, jealous of Christ's popularity, as an excuse to bring Him before the Roman magistrate on charges of treason. These religious leaders conspired to bring false charges against Christ for blasphemy because He "claimed to be equal with God." Christ was seized and taken before a religious court, where false witnesses accused Him of treason against God.

Eventually, in fulfillment of the Old Testament Scriptures, the Messiah Jesus was brought before Pilate, the Roman governor of Judea, and ultimately was condemned to be crucified—a cruel mode of executing convicted prisoners. Although Christ Jesus was sinless, He did not die in vain. Through His death on the cross, Christ paid for the sins of His chosen people. After Jesus died, He was placed in a tomb that was sealed by a huge stone and guarded by several Roman soldiers day and night. On the third day after His death, in spite of the sealed tomb and Roman guards, Christ arose from the dead; demonstrating His great power over sin and death. He also appeared in bodily form to hundreds of His followers. Reports soon spread far and wide concerning Christ's resurrection and ascension to heaven, but many of the Roman and Jewish people had difficulty believing these reports.

The teachings of Jesus seemed very strange to the men of the Roman world. The Greeks and the Romans believed that there were many gods, whom they tried to please by offering sacrifices. Jesus taught that there is but one God, and that the way to please Him is by serving Him wholeheartedly ac-

The Messiah, Jesus Christ, came to the earth during the reign of Caesar Augustus and He was tried by a Roman governor named Pilate during the rule of Tiberius.

cording to His commandments. He taught, "You shall love the Lord your God with all your heart, with all your soul and with all your mind. This is the first and great commandment. And the second is like it: You shall love your neighbor as yourself" (Matthew 22:37–39). Love to God, must be first, and then love to others. Jesus gave the world its finest rule of conduct when He said, "Therefore, whatever you want men to do to you, do also to them" (Matthew 7:12a).

Jesus was the first teacher of real liberty in the world. Although many of the ancient Greek cities had democratic governments, only a small body of citizens had a part in them. In every Greek city, there were many slaves and other residents who had no voice in the government. The teachings of Christ elevated the status of all manner of men and gave dignity to people who were honest, hardworking, and yet poor. He taught that the true role of leaders is to serve others with compassion and humility. This means that all rulers will be judged according to how justly they used the power loaned to them by Almighty God. Jesus Christ also taught that true liberty is not the right to live as we please, but the power to live as God requires. The Gospel of Christ has the power to free people from the bondage of sin.

The religions of Greece and Rome did little to teach men to be good or to do right. Jesus taught that all men everywhere ought to be good. In His own pure and unselfish life He gave the world its highest ideal of character. His teachings have, sadly, never been fully adopted, even in Christian countries. The best of men fall far short of following closely in His footsteps. But in spite of man's sinfulness, Christ's life and His Gospel have been the greatest influence in developing the legacy of liberty that has often characterized Western culture.

The Beginnings of the Church

At the time of Christ's death and resurrection, He had only a few hundred followers or disciples. The first converts to the Christian religion were made in Jerusalem and in the other parts of Judea. At first, it was thought that the new faith was intended only for the Jews. Then the Apostle Peter, a prominent leader among the apostles, taught that the message of salvation through faith in the Lord Jesus Christ was for all peoples.

Among the early converts to the Christian faith was a Jewish tentmaker and Pharisee, Saul of Tarsus. After he became a Christian he was called Paul. This gifted man did more than anyone else to make Christianity a religion for all manner of men. For thirty years he traveled far and wide in Asia Minor, Greece, and Italy, telling the story of Jesus with burning forcefulness through the power and grace of the Holy Spirit. Before his death he had gathered together, in many of the cities of the Roman Empire, church groups made up of men and women who were faithful followers of Christ seeking to live the Christian life in obedience to the teachings of the Holy Scripture.

Paul, a Roman citizen and one of Jesus' most dedicated servants, is here preaching the Gospel to the poor. Many became Christians in the latter days of the Roman Empire.

Paul wrote letters to many of the churches that he had founded, explaining the teachings of Jesus as given to him by God the Holy Spirit. The primary message that the Apostle Paul emphasized was the need for sinful men to repent from their sins and to seek salvation through faith in the atoning work of Christ on the Cross.

Four different accounts of the life and work of Jesus were also written. These narratives and letters, with a few other early Christian writings, make up the portion of the Bible known as the New Testament.

At first the Christian churches were little groups of believers, who met to worship together. The Christians of each community thought of themselves as brothers and gave freely of their property to support the widows, the poor, and the sick in their midst. Paul the Apostle taught that certain men should be appointed in each church as leaders to attend to the necessary business. Those who took care of the property and looked after the needs of the poor were called deacons. The leaders in each church, who taught the other members and administered the biblical sacraments of baptism and communion, were called bishops or elders. Leaders in the early Christian church were often married and continued to earn their own living just as the rest of the church members did.

The Romans Persecute the Christians

From the Church's beginning, the faith of the Christians was tried by persecution. Jesus, its great Founder, was crucified. Stephen, the first martyr, was stoned to death. Nearly all the twelve apostles paid for their faith with their lives. Paul, the "Apostle to the Gentiles," was attacked again and again, and at last his life was taken as he was beheaded in Rome.

When the Christian faith began to spread over the Roman world, the pagan people in most regions hated it. There were some reasons for this feeling. The Romans believed in a great many gods. For example, one of their gods presided over war and another over commerce. They had one goddess who watched the flocks and another who caused the grain to ripen. The Romans were willing to add the God of the Christians to those that they already worshipped, but they were not willing to throw away their own gods. This, however, was the very thing that the Christians demanded. They declared that the gods of

The leaders of Rome sponsored exciting and deadly spectacles in their Coliseum to amuse and pacify their disgruntled citizens. As Rome became more pagan and decadent, the people began to call for more bloody games. During the rise of Christianity, thousands of Christians who had been accused of disloyalty because they refused to worship and follow Caesar were tortured and killed in the Coliseum.

Rome were false gods and that they must not be worshipped. Consequently, they refused to do anything that would honor or even recognize the gods of Rome. They also refused to worship the Roman emperor as a god as the law required. They would not attend the religious feasts or entertainments of the time, nor go to the fights of the gladiators, nor even send their children to pagan Roman schools. Because the Christians thus refused to join in the social and religious life of the people around them, they were called "haters of mankind." It is not strange that such people were misunderstood by many of the carnal and worldly people of Rome.

The Roman people feared the Christians almost as much as they disliked them. All sorts of false stories were told about the awful things they did in their secret meetings. If any great disaster happened, the Christians were thought to have caused it. One of the early Christian writers reveals, "If the Tiber rises, if the Nile does not rise, if the heavens give no rain, if there is an earthquake, famine, or pestilence straightway the cry is 'The Christians to the lions.'"

For a time, at first, the followers of Christ had attracted little attention from the Roman government. The emperors did not care what the Christians believed for they were regarded as merely a strange sect of Judaism. But when they learned that the Christians scorned the gods of the nation, would not serve in the army, and were holding secret meetings contrary to the law, they decided to suppress them by force.

On a regular basis, for nearly three hundred years, the Christians were persecuted throughout the empire. During this time there were thousands of victims. Some were tortured in every way that their cruel persecutors could invent. Many were beheaded, or burned, or crucified. Great numbers were thrown to the wild beasts in the great Coliseum at Rome.

In facing this awful persecution, the early Christians gave us the greatest example of heroic courage, fortitude in suffering, and unfaltering devotion to Christ in all the history of the world. When Blandina, a young girl, was tortured from morning until night to force her to give up her faith, she continued steadfast in saying, "I am a Christian; among us no evil is done." When the aged bishop, Polycarp, was commanded to curse Christ, he answered, "Six and eighty years have I served Him, and He has done me nothing but good, and how could I curse Him, my Lord and my Savior!"

Instead of crushing out the religion of Christ, persecution only strengthened it and caused it to spread. The Christians who suffered were called *martyrs*, that means "witnesses." The martyrs were steadily convincing people of the truth of a faith whose followers willingly and even joyously gave their lives to defend. It was true, as one of the early Christians said, "The blood of the martyrs became the seed of the church."

The people of Rome loved to watch the chariot races held at the arena within their impressive Coliseum.

The Triumph of the Church

The persecution of the Christians was most severe in the third century. Yet it was just at that time that the followers of Christ were increasing more rapidly than ever before. The inspiring influence of the martyrs was not the only reason for this growth. At a time when men were losing faith in the old gods of Greece and Rome, the Christians were filled with zeal and energy. Multitudes of people turned eagerly to a faith that taught them to be loving and helpful to each other in this life and gave them a sure hope of a better life in another world.

The existence of the Roman Empire itself helped the missionaries of the new faith to do their work. Its splendid roads gave ready access to every part of the known world. The fact that both the Latin and Greek languages were known and used everywhere made it easy to preach the Christian message to all people. By building up its empire, Rome had prepared the way for the rapid growth of Christianity.

One of the important accomplishments of the Roman empire was the establishment of good roads throughout many parts of southern Europe. Some of their roads were so well built that they were actively used for almost two thousand years.

The story is told that as the emperor Constantine was going into battle he saw a cross of light in the sky with these words upon it: "In this sign thou shalt conquer." Constantine won the battle, and soon afterward, early in the fourth century, he issued an order saying, "We grant to the Christians and to all others free choice to follow the mode of worship they may wish." From that time, the persecution of the Christians ceased.

After it met with the favor of the emperor, Christianity spread more rapidly than ever. Great numbers of people soon accepted it. Belief in the gods of Greece and Rome steadily passed away. Before the end of the fourth century, another emperor prohibited the old pagan worship under pain of death. All the pagan temples were then torn down or changed into Christian churches.

This triumph of the Christian Church was a long step forward in God's plan to redeem the world through Jesus Christ. It also opened a new era of better living in the world. The orphans, the poor, and the sick are far better cared for in Christian countries than in pagan lands. After Christianity became the religion of the Roman Empire the slaves were better treated, many of them were freed, and the brutal and bloody "games" of the gladiators were finally stopped.

When gladiators were abused, idle Romans were amused.

While Christianity was winning its way in the Roman Empire, the organization of the Church was developing. In the course of time, the bishops in the great cities like Alexandria, Antioch, Constantinople, Jerusalem, and Rome came to be looked upon as the leaders in the Church. After the emperors made Christianity the religion of the empire, most of these bishops became officers of the state. They were no longer poor and persecuted, but rich and powerful.

As Christianity developed under the emperors, the authority of the Church, which formerly had rested in the hands of local or regional bishops, became more centralized. Over a period of years, the newfound wealth and popularity of Christianity brought corruption into the leadership of the Church at Rome. In an effort to further expand their power base in the world, the Church at Rome ruled that the bishop of Rome should be called the pope; and after the Western Roman Empire fell, he became the most influential person in Europe. Rome had so long been the capital of the world that it was natural for people to receive commands from it. Moreover, the missionaries sent out by the bishop of Rome had done so much to help the common man that many people from southern Europe looked up to him with affection and loyalty.

CHAPTER SUMMARY

Shortly before the birth of Christ, a powerful empire developed in the city of Rome that steadily grew to dominate much of Europe, North Africa, and the Middle East. For hundreds of years, the Roman armies conquered many nations and subdued many barbarian tribes. In addition, the leaders from Rome organized many building projects and created a system of roads that helped to advance commerce and unite their empire. At the height of Rome's power, around A.D. 150, it was often said, "all roads lead to Rome."

For hundreds of years, the Roman armies were able to subdue and conquer many barbarian tribes throughout much of Europe. The mighty legions, however, did not remain invincible forever.

As time went on, the Roman government and people became corrupt and immoral and began to lose control over their vast empire. Eventually, Germanic tribes called the Goths overthrew the Western Roman Empire in 476 A.D. The once proud Romans with their impressive buildings, powerful monarchs, and mighty military legions were destroyed along with the civil order that they maintained. Almost im-

The barbarian tribes that overran Rome stole property and burned most of the city. The fall of the Roman Empire permitted the lawless barbarians to destroy much of European culture and start the period known as the Dark Ages.

mediately, chaos began to develop across much of the former Roman Empire in Western Europe. The same barbarian tribes that sacked Rome were utterly incapable of maintaining law and order. In fact, these Germanic tribes often fought with each other as the darkness of anarchy and confusion spread throughout Western Europe.

When the Roman Empire began, at the perfect time in human history, the Son of God, Jesus Christ, came to this world. Christ came to redeem all those whom the Father had given to Him, by making atonement for their sins through the shedding of His own blood on the Cross. After Christ arose bodily from the dead, He appeared many times to His followers over a space of forty days. Before Christ ascended unto Heaven, He promised that He would send God the Holy Spirit to empower His followers to take the Gospel of Christ into the entire world. This was the beginning of the Christian Church in the New Testament era.

Early on, the leaders of Rome went from ignoring Christians to persecuting them openly. Thousands of faithful and courageous Christians were murdered or harassed. As the Roman Empire began to decline, however, more and more people began to embrace the message of salvation in Christ and the Christian Church grew to the point where it was no longer an outlawed religion.

The old Roman Empire was broken up into several smaller countries. Most of these countries are still in existence today.

Chapter Questions and Activities

1. How many years ago was the city of Rome founded?

2. In what year did the Roman Empire split into East and West?

3. Why did people during this time say that "all roads lead to Rome"?

4. Find out how roads were made during Roman times and compare that to the roads of today.

5. Who was the founder of the Christian Church?

6. Who was the Apostle Paul and what did he do to spread Christianity?

7. Look up some information about the famous martyr named Polycarp.

8. Did Christianity stay an outlawed religion in Rome?

9. Why did Rome grow weaker in the days of the last emperors?

Key Terms

Persecute	Magistrate
Barbarian	Atonement
Constantinople	Commerce

Chapter 3
THE FRANKS & CHARLEMAGNE

THE GERMANIC TRIBES

North of Italy, in Central Europe, there lived a warlike race of people called the Germans. Many different tribes made up the Germanic race, one of which we called the Teutons. The Germans were not Christians but worshiped the same false gods—Odin, Frigga, Thor, and many others—as the Vikings. Odin and Frigga were the king and queen of the Germanic gods, and Thor was the mighty god of thunder.

The Germans were tall, powerful men with blond hair and blue eyes, very different from the dark-haired, dark-eyed men of Rome. They wore rough clothes made of wool and lived in huts made of stone or baked mud with roofs of matted straw. When they moved to new lands they took with them their herds of sheep and cattle. Wherever they settled they planted patches of wheat, barley, and flax.

A separate warlike group called the Huns lived in what is now called Russia. They were even more warlike than the Germans. When bands of Huns began coming into the lands of the Germans, the Germanic tribes were forced to move out. Many of them moved into the Western Roman Empire. Some forced their way into Spain, some into Gaul, and others into Italy and North Africa.

Germanic tribes came from eastern Europe and parts of Scandinavia and settled in many regions in central Europe. These simple people were often illiterate, warlike, and uncivilized. The once mighty Roman Empire was eventually overcome by a united group of Germanic tribes.

The Germanic tribes, which moved into Spain and into Italy, were known as the Goths. When these tribes began sweeping into Italy, burning buildings and killing or carrying off people, the weakened Roman armies could not stop them. As you already learned, the city of Rome was overrun in A.D. 410 and eventually, in 476, the Western Roman Empire came to an end. The Eastern Roman Empire, however, continued on for almost a thousand years.

Armed with superior weapons, Roman soldiers fought in well-formed battle lines. How are the barbarians fighting in this drawing?

The Dark Ages

The fall of the Western Roman Empire was followed by a period of about five hundred years, during which many of the people of Western Europe were ignorant and poor and led miserable lives. This period is called the *Dark Ages.*

The Germans were herdsmen and did not care to live in cities. After they invaded the Western Roman Empire, Rome and the other cities of the empire began to fall into ruins. The Roman roads were neglected. Large vessels were no longer built to sail upon the sea. Most of the beautiful Roman paintings and statues were lost or destroyed. The art of writing was almost forgotten, and education practically stopped. Without a trained army to keep order, there was constant fighting between the different tribes of Germans. Robbers ruled the roads, and neither the life nor the property of any person was safe.

Toward the end of the Dark Ages, conditions grew better. The Germanic people gradually learned many things from the Romans. Some of them even began to live in the old cities with the Romans, and others built towns of their own. They borrowed words from Latin, the language of Rome, and added them to their own speech. They also adopted some of the teachings and laws of the Christian church and made other laws of their own. Governments were formed, and once more there were armies to keep order.

A Germanic chief has called an assembly of warriors who are eager to fight against the cruel and harsh rule of the Romans.

In some ways the Germanic people even improved upon the Roman way of living. They lived a much simpler and more wholesome life. They were a freedom-loving people; and in the governments that they established, they had a say in choosing their leaders and in deciding matters of public importance. The Germans respected women more than any of the ancient European peoples had, because they had come under the influence of Christian missionaries sent out from monasteries throughout Europe. The mixing of the strong and vigorous Germans with the Roman people produced a new race, which in many ways was better than either the German or the Roman races had been.

Roman power long stabilized the ancient world.

The Franks

One of the Germanic tribes that invaded the Western Roman Empire was known as the Franks. They crossed the Rhine River and settled in Gaul—modern day France. At first, these Franks were divided into many little tribes, each ruled by its own king and fighting its own battles with its own small army. No one of these tribes was very strong.

Clovis

In the year A.D. 481, the king of one of the tribes of Franks in northern Gaul died and his son Clovis took his place. Though Clovis was only fifteen years old when he became king, he was a natural leader. During the thirty years in which Clovis ruled, he brought all of the little tribes of Franks under his leadership.

There is an interesting story told of Clovis. When first he was king, he worshiped the many false gods of the Franks. His wife was a Christian; that is, she repented from sin, believed that Christ purchased salvation for her on the cross and would save her soul from sin and eternal death. One day, while Clovis was leading his army against a neighboring tribe, he saw that his men were being badly beaten. He prayed to his gods for help, but still his men fell back before the enemy.

Seeing a cross in the sky, Clovis remembered that his wife had often urged him to give up the worship of his gods and to become a Christian. Here was an opportunity to try out the Christian God. Raising his arms to heaven, he vowed that, if God would help him win the battle, he would become a Christian. The battle went on and the army of Clovis finally won. True to his promise, the king became a Christian. On Christmas day in the year 496, he was baptized, together with 3,000 of his men. The people of his kingdom followed his example; and, from that time on, the Franks were a Christian people.

When Clovis first became king in 481, his kingdom was very small. It included only a little land around the city of Paris in northern Gaul. Before his death, he had extended his kingdom east beyond the Rhine River and almost as far south as Spain. The Franks and the Romans in this land came to speak the same language, a mixture of German and Latin words, which became the French language of today. Little by little, these people were united into one nation, whose land was known as the kingdom of the Franks. After the death of Clovis, his kingdom was divided among his four sons, and for a long time the Franks were poorly ruled.

Charles Martel and the Moors

In northern Africa, a dark-skinned people known as the Moors lived and worked. They were not Christians but followed the teachings of a false prophet named Muhammad, and they were known as Muslims, or people who submit to Allah, or God. The Moors were brave and skilled fighters who desired to destroy Christian civilization in North Africa and in other lands. Muhammad taught his followers that Allah called them to a holy war, or *jihad*, against those who oppose their religion.

In the year 711, the Moors sent an army from Africa into Spain. The Goths who were living in Spain fought hard against them but were soon defeated, and it was not long before the whole Spanish peninsula was in the hands of the Moors. For a while, these conquerors lived there peacefully, establishing their religion and their civilization. They built many fine buildings, the most famous of which was the

Alhambra—the palace and fortress of the Moorish monarchs—in the city of Granada. Then, wishing for more lands to conquer, they sent an army across the Pyrenees Mountains into the kingdom of the Franks.

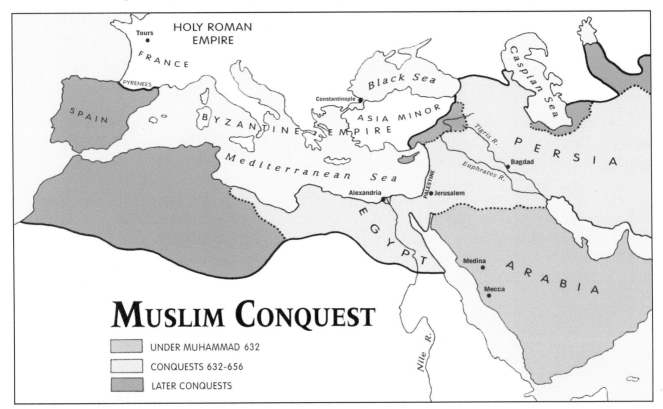

An able leader of the Franks, named Charles Martel, led his army against the invaders. He met them at a place called Tours. So strong was Charles Martel and so heavy were the blows which he struck in battle, that he was known to his followers as Charles the Hammer. After a fierce struggle, the Moors were defeated and driven back into Spain, never to return. The battle of Tours was one of the most important battles in all history. If the Franks had lost, the Moors would surely have conquered most of western Europe and spread the Muslim religion in place of the Christian faith.

In the time of Charles Martel, the king of the Franks was a weak ruler, and Martel gained great power and really ruled the kingdom. He was content to let the king keep his title so long as he, himself, had the power. Martel's son, Pepin III, however, had different ideas. After his father's death he made himself king of the Franks. It was a good thing for the Franks that this happened, for Pepin's son, who ruled after him, proved to be the greatest ruler the Franks ever had.

The followers of Muhammad were skilled fighters. They killed many groups of people in their quest to spread the religion of Islam.

Charlemagne

Pepin's son, Charlemagne, or Charles the Great, declared himself king in the year 751, after dethroning the weak king of the Franks. After his father died in 768, the kingdom was divided between Charles and his younger brother Carloman, which was the custom. On Carloman's sudden death, however, Charlemagne made himself the sole ruler of the Franks.

Charlemagne lived very simply. He did not try to make himself seem better than other men. He wore the same kind of clothes that his people wore. He did not eat or drink too much, nor give expensive entertainments. In fact, he set a wonderful example for the people of his kingdom to follow.

Charlemagne was not only a skilled military leader but also a wise political leader. He helped to organize schools for young people and to establish a standard for written communication.

Charlemagne, however, was not well educated. He was a grown man before he learned to read, and he never learned to write much more than his own name. Still, he believed in education and did a great deal toward increasing the knowledge of his people. He founded many schools and brought to them the best teachers from other countries. One of these schools was called "The School of the Palace." Here the children of his court studied; sometimes the king himself attended the school.

It is said that Charlemagne once visited a school in his kingdom and found the poor boys studying hard and learning their lessons well. The rich boys, however, who were the sons of nobles and other wealthy people of the kingdom, were not studying. They were wasting their time with games and other pleasures. Charlemagne was much displeased. After scolding these boys well, he told them that if they did not stop wasting time and did not study their lessons they could never expect any help or favors from him.

Charlemagne was fond of rare and beautiful things, and, during his reign, painters, sculptors, and metal workers began once more to work at their art, which had been neglected since the fall of Rome. Builders also began to copy the old Roman buildings, and the palaces and cathedrals which they erected were the best that had been built in Europe since the fall of the Western Roman Empire.

Being a Christian, Charlemagne was anxious to do all he could to strengthen and spread the Christian faith. So he built a fine cathedral, numerous churches, and several monasteries, or homes for the monks. The monks were men who believed that the pleasures of the world were spiritually distracting and often sinful. They lived apart from other people and devoted their lives to worshiping God, to study, to teaching, and to making copies of the greatest book of all time—the Holy Bible.

The Influence of the Monks

The monks did much to help the tribes of barbarians to learn civilized ways of living. They were the earliest missionaries of the Christian faith to the pagans. Wherever they settled, they built monasteries and became teachers of industry as well as of religion. They cleared the land, drained the bogs, built roads and bridges, and by their example taught the people the best ways of farming known in their time. In many

Young people often helped to work the land as farmhands in ancient times. How have farming techniques changed over the years? Do young people still work as farmhands?

of the monasteries, there were monks who worked at the various trades and so kept the knowledge of the manual arts and crafts—which the Romans possessed—from being lost in the Middle Ages.

In the same way, many of the books and some of the art of Greece and Rome were preserved during the centuries of confusion and turmoil which followed the fall of the Roman Empire. Every monastery had a writing room in which the monks copied and illustrated such books as they possessed. For a long time, nearly all the schools in Western Europe were in the monasteries. At their doors, the poor, the sick, and the hungry commonly received help and comfort. The weary traveler normally found hospitable shelter under their roofs. In a word, the monks taught the world many a needed lesson in labor, learning, self-denial, and charity. Although most of the early monasteries were loosely connected to the bishop at Rome, many were independent and locally controlled.

The burden of maintaining libraries and schools of knowledge during the Middle Ages fell upon the Church. Monks spent much of their time copying worthwhile books and teaching pupils.

At first men entered the monasteries in order to escape from the temptations in the world, to live quiet and peaceful lives, and to save their own souls. But in the later Middle Ages, when the vast majority of monasteries were under the firm control of the Roman Catholic Church, a new order of monks arose whose members—called *friars*, which meant "brothers"—went about in the world preaching to people and helping the poor and the sick.

The church was the greatest civilizing influence in the Middle Ages. Although some of the doctrines of the Christian Church became corrupted or perverted during this era, the Church continued on and handed down to us most of our knowledge of the education, literature, and art of the Greeks and the Romans.

In nearly every city of Europe where a bishop of the church lived in the Middle Ages, there stands today a beautiful building called a cathedral. These vast cathedrals, with their splendid windows filled with beautiful stained glass and paintings, tell of the love and devotion which the people who built them possessed. The cathedrals of the Middle Ages are among the noblest works of art in the entire world.

After the collapse of the Roman government, the Church took over many of the functions of civil society and became very powerful. The Church built many monasteries staffed by abbots and monks. They also had vast land holdings. Many conflicts arose during the Middle Ages between officials from the Church at Rome and secular princes or kings.

In order to spread the Christian religion, Charlemagne sent out many missionaries, or messengers of God, to neighboring countries. Sometimes he also sent out armies to overcome pagan tribes and make them accept the Christian religion. There were many robbers in those days; and, in order to protect church property and church people, Charlemagne made the punishment for robbing churches and monasteries very severe.

Charlemagne's Laws and Courts

Charlemagne did much for his people besides encouraging education and art and spreading the Christian religion. He made and enforced many just laws. He was wise enough not to insist that all of the tribes over whom he ruled should be governed by the same set of laws. Each tribe was allowed to keep its own laws, provided they were just and reasonable. All of the laws were copied down; and, once each year, the king called together all of the warriors in his kingdom to discuss them. At these meetings, the laws were read aloud and the warriors were permitted to make suggestions about new laws that were needed or old laws that should be changed or given up. The king, however, was the only one who could actually change the laws.

In order to be sure that his laws were being obeyed and that justice was being done, Charlemagne had law courts throughout his kingdom. He also sent out special messengers, who traveled about and reported to him all cases which they found where the laws were not obeyed.

Charlemagne's Wars

In the forty-four years of his reign, Charlemagne carried on many wars against different enemies. Often he himself led his armies into battle. He fought against the Lombards, a warlike tribe living in northern Italy, and made their whole country a part of his kingdom. He conquered the Germanic tribes and the Avars of the Danube valley, forcing them to become Christians. Charlemagne even led an army into Spain to fight the Moors. Though he was unsuccessful in his first invasion of Spain and was forced to return to his kingdom, he later conquered part of northern Spain. Before his death, Charlemagne had greatly enlarged his kingdom.

This map shows the extent of the empire ruled by Charlemagne and the route taken by the Vikings into the city of Constantinople.

The Story of Roland

A famous story is told about Charlemagne's first invasion of Spain. With the army was Roland, a brave young soldier, the son of Charlemagne's sister. Supposedly, Roland's stepfather, Ganelon, was chosen by Charlemagne to negotiate the peace treaty with the enemy. At once, Ganelon became enraged because Roland was the one who suggested that Ganelon be sent on the dangerous mission. Two previous ambassadors had been brutally murdered on such a mission. Ganelon, therefore, schemed with the enemy to have Roland destroyed. When the Franks started to return home, Ganelon arranged for his stepson to be placed in command of the soldiers who guarded the rear of the army. It was Roland's duty to hold off the enemy if they should try to attack the army from behind. He had a horn, though, that he was to blow if the enemy proved to be too strong and the rear guard needed help.

As Roland and his men entered a narrow mountain pass, the Moors fell upon them. The Franks fought bravely, but they were greatly outnumbered. Roland's comrade Oliver continually persuaded him to blow the horn, but the young leader was too proud to call for help when there was still a chance of winning. The battle went on; and, one after another, the Franks fell before the enemy. Still Roland would not blow his horn. At last, only a few of his men were left.

Then, with all his strength, Roland blew a mighty blast. Faintly the sound came to Charlemagne, riding at the head of his army far away. Back rode the king and his men. They were in time to keep the Moors from coming through the pass but not in time to save Roland, Oliver, and his gallant band. Surrounded by the bodies of hundreds of their enemies, Roland and every one of his men lay dead.

When Charlemagne returned home, he told Aude—Roland's betrothed, who was also Oliver's sister—the tragic story. The shock of the dreadful news was too much for poor Aude; and, in despair, she fell dead at Charlemagne's feet. The truth about Roland's stepfather was finally revealed, and Ganelon was put on trial and sentenced to death. The stepfather's treachery against Roland not only injured the king but the French nation, for Ganelon had committed treason.

Charlemagne Is Made Emperor

In the year 800 A.D., Charlemagne went to Rome to help settle a church dispute. The pope, who had asked him to come, was believed by many to be the highest officer of the Christian Church. On Christmas day, as Charlemagne knelt in prayer at St. Peter's Church in Rome, the pope set a crown upon his head and announced that Charlemagne was now "The Great and Peaceful Emperor of the Romans." Charlemagne was surprised, but he accepted his new title.

Although Charlemagne was not a Roman but a Frank, the pope had a very good reason for calling him "the Emperor of the Romans." Ever since the fall of the Western Roman Empire more than three hundred years before, the Eastern Roman Empire had continued to be powerful. The pope was very anxious to establish a new Western Roman Empire to take the place of the one that the Germans had destroyed. If this were done, he believed that the Eastern and Western Roman Empires might once more be brought together under a single government with Rome as the capital city.

The year after Charlemagne was crowned, he tried to unite his new empire and the Eastern Roman Empire under one government. A woman, the Empress Irene, then ruled the Eastern Roman Empire.

Charlemagne sent messengers to Constantinople to ask the empress if she would accept him as her husband. Before the match could be arranged, however, the people of the Eastern Empire revolted and drove Irene from the throne. In her place they put an emperor who did not want to make the two empires into one. The plan, therefore, came to nothing.

The End of Charlemagne's Empire

Charlemagne realized that his empire could not exist long after his death, so he arranged to have it divided equally among his three sons. Two of the sons, however, died before their father, so the whole empire was left to the third son. Though he was a weak ruler he managed to hold the empire together during his reign, and at his death it was left to his own three sons. For a short time they fought with each other but at last a treaty was made and the empire was divided into three parts. In time, these three parts became three strong and independent countries—France, Germany, and Italy.

WHAT THE GERMANIC PEOPLE GAVE US

• The idea that each man should be free to express his opinion about matters of public importance.

• The idea that women should be treated with respect.

• The idea that there is dignity in working the land as a farmer or herdsman.

CHAPTER SUMMARY

The powerful city of Rome once ruled all of western and southern Europe and many countries of Asia and Africa. In time, Rome lost her strength and the empire was divided into the Eastern Roman Empire and the Western Roman Empire.

As Rome grew weaker, warlike Germanic tribes from central Europe invaded the Western Roman Empire. At last, they conquered the city of Rome; and, in A.D. 476, the Western Roman Empire came to an end.

For over five hundred years after the fall of the Western Roman Empire, most of the people of western Europe were ignorant, poor, and miserable. This period is known as the Dark Ages. Toward the end of the Dark Ages conditions grew better as the barbarian tribes learned many things from the Romans and from Christian missionaries.

The Germanic tribes who settled in Gaul were called Franks. King Clovis united all the little tribes of Franks into one nation. He also made the Franks a Christian people.

In northern Africa lived a dark-skinned people known as the Moors. They were Muslims. In the year 711, the Moors conquered Spain. When they sent an army into the kingdom of the Franks they were defeated by Charles Martel in the battle of Tours and driven back into Spain.

Charles Martel never became king of the Franks, but his son, Pepin III, did. Pepin's son, who followed him on the throne, was known as Charles the Great, or Charlemagne.

Charlemagne was the greatest king of the Franks. He encouraged education by founding schools. He built a cathedral and many churches and monasteries, and spread the Christian religion to neighboring tribes. He made good laws for his kingdom and established courts to enforce them. He fought many wars and greatly enlarged his kingdom. In A.D. 800, Charlemagne was crowned Emperor of the Romans.

After Charlemagne's death, his son ruled his empire. When the son died, the empire was left to his three sons. For a short time they quarreled but at last the empire was divided into three parts, which in time became the three countries of France, Germany, and Italy.

CHAPTER QUESTIONS AND ACTIVITIES

1. Who were the Germans? Why were they important?

2. What were the Dark Ages?

3. In what ways did the Germanic people improve upon the Roman civilization?

4. Who were the Franks?

5. Who was Clovis, and what did he do?

6. Tell how Clovis became a Christian.

7. What did Charles Martel do that helped the Franks?

8. Who was Pepin? What did he do?

9. In what ways did Charlemagne set an example for the people of his kingdom to follow?

10. What did Charlemagne do for education?

11. How did Charlemagne spread the Christian religion?

12. Visit a court of law in your community and try to learn why we need laws and justice.

13. Name several tribes conquered by Charlemagne.

14. Tell the story of Roland.

15. How was Charlemagne made Emperor of the Romans?

16. What happened to Charlemagne's empire after his death?

17. What three ideas have come down to us from the Germans?

KEY TERMS

Herdsmen	Gallant
Repent	Moors
Sculptor	Treaty

CHRIST VS. THE QUR'AN

Who are the Muslims?

Many wrongly believe that all Arabs are Muslims, but many are Christians. For example, in the Arab Republic of Egypt, an estimated ten percent of the population, or about five million, claim the name of Christ. Even so, the majority of Arabs are Muslims who live, not only in Saudi Arabia, but also in other countries around the world; only fifteen percent of Muslims, though, are of Arab descent. In fact, Muslims hail from many other nations—from Morocco to Indonesia.

The name *Muslim* means "one who submits." A Muslim, therefore, is a person who submits to *Allah*, or "God," and believes that Muhammad is his prophet. The Muslim's religion is called *Islam*, which means "submission [to God]," as set forth in the Muslim holy book, called the Qur'an (also spelled, Koran). The basic duties of a Muslim are called the Five Pillars of Islam: the recitation of their creed, daily prayers, the giving of alms, the fast of Ramadan, and the pilgrimage to Mecca.

One more sacred duty of Islam needs to be addressed: the duty of *jihad*, or "holy war." All adult Muslim men are required to answer the call to war against the *infidels*, or "those who reject Islam." If a Muslim dies in a jihad, he is guaranteed a place in paradise. From the beginning, Muslims have divided the world into *Dar al-Islam*, the House of Islam, and *Dar al-Harb*, the House of War—where the rule of Islam should be extended, if necessary by war. As a result, radical Islamic leaders have emerged, such as Saddam Hussein and Osama bin Laden, advocating terrorism against all infidels—especially those who have taken land from the House of Islam (e.g., Israel) or have supported them (e.g., the United States).

At first glance, Islam and Christianity seem to have many things in common. Both believe in one God, who created the universe. Both have developed advances in science, medicine, and mathematics. Even during the Middle Ages, Muslims encouraged medical research because Muhammad taught "God has not created an illness without creating a cure for it." Both religions oppose homosexuality and abortion. And both accept followers from all national and ethnic backgrounds. The truth is, however, that Christians and Muslims do not worship the same God. In fact, Muslims do not worship the true God at all.

"Of all the major religions of the world, Islam is the only one which is definitely anti-Christian at its core. Since its rise in the seventh century, Islam has spread mostly at the expense of Christian lands."[1] By the time of Muhammad, the Gospel had spread throughout the known world, from Spain to India, but the early Church failed to declare the true message of the Bible to their Arab neighbors. In fact, Arabs seldom heard the Gospel until hundreds of years after Muhammad established Islam in the Arabian Peninsula. Not until the nineteenth century did Christian missions begin to proclaim the Gospel to Muslims.

What do Muslims believe?

Muslims think very highly of *Isa* or, "Jesus," believing in his virgin birth and even calling him "a spirit from God." According to the Qur'an, Isa was a miracle worker who was pure and sinless, but he is never spoken of as the Son of God. The Qur'an also states that Isa died, but not on the cross because Muhammad thought such a death was too humiliating. Even so, he is now in heaven and, one day, will return to Earth to win adherents to Islam before he dies once again.

Muslims also do not think they need a Savior because, to them, *sins* are simply "mistakes" that flow out of human weakness. Such weakness can be overcome by fulfilling the requirements of the *sharia*, or the "law." Since Islam is essentially a religion of good works, Muslims seek to appease Allah by worshiping him and submitting to his law. Islam denies original sin and teaches that man is essentially good, having the ability to reach perfection if one follows the rules.

The false god of Islam is a harsh deity who knows only submission, but the true God of Scripture is both just and merciful. The Qur'an speaks of a severe master who allows believers to be his servants, but the Bible speaks of a loving God who adopts believers into His family. Muslims respect Isa as a prophet, but Christians trust Christ as God's one and only Son who died on the cross to redeem them from their sins.

How can Muslims know Christ?

Muslims believe that the eternal words of Allah came down from heaven in the form of the Qur'an, so it is important to tell them that the true eternal Word of God came to Earth in the form of our Lord and Savior, Jesus Christ. Salvation only comes through Him—the sinless God-man who came to seek and to save the lost.

Muslims are seeking for the truth, and Jesus is that Truth (John 14:6). God's Truth reveals that all are in need of a Savior because all have sinned and fall short of God's glory (Romans 3:23). Moreover, as the Apostle Paul writes, "For the wages of sin is death, but the gift of God is eternal life in Christ Jesus our Lord" (Romans 6:23). A person is saved by grace, through faith; thus salvation is a gift of God—not of human effort or good works, so no one can boast (Ephesians 2:8, 9).

---

[1] Bassam M. Madany, *Sharing God's Word with a Muslim* (Palos Heights, IL: The Back to God Hour, 1981), page 1.

Chapter 4
THE NORTHMEN, OR VIKINGS

"Skoal to the Northmen! Skoal!" So shouted the listeners long ago as the story-tellers of a far northern land recited the daring deeds of their famous heroes. "*Skoal!*" means "Hail!" and well might the eager listeners cheer their heroes, for the Northmen, or Vikings, were the most adventurous and daring of any of the old-time peoples.

The Norse People

In the northern lands of Europe, where Norway, Sweden, and Denmark now are, there once lived a wild and daring people. These were the Northmen, or Norsemen, as they were also called. The Northmen, like the Goths and Franks who overran the Western Roman Empire, belonged to the Germanic race and were often fierce and barbaric.

The soil of the Norse country was thin and rocky and so was not well suited for raising crops. The winters were long and the summers short. In their need for food, the Northmen turned to the forests, where there were many wild animals, and to the nearby seas, where the fishing was good.

The many deep bays along the Norse coasts made splendid harbors, and the vast northern forests supplied wood for building ships. At first the Northmen made little fishing boats, in which they rowed out to spread their nets in the waters of the bays. As time went on, larger and more seaworthy boats were made, capable of traveling long distances in rough water. Gradually the Northmen became a nation of skilled and daring sailors. Far out in the North Sea, they discovered richer fishing grounds than those near home.

For hundreds of years, the Northmen lived peacefully in their northern lands, depending on the sea for most of their living. Each spring, when the waters were clear of ice, the men from the Norse settlements would climb into their boats and sail out to the fishing grounds. The wives and children stayed behind in little villages and worked hard in the fields to raise what crops they could. From time to time, the fishing boats would return laden with fish, which the women and children cleaned and prepared for food. Some of the fish were dried for use during the long cold winters. After a few days at home, the fishing boats would sail away again on another fishing trip. This is the way the Northmen lived during the spring, summer, and fall.

During the winter, the harbors were choked with ice and the men could no longer carry on their trade of fishing. Then the boats, nets, and weapons were repaired and new ones made. In the evenings, the men gathered in long wooden halls lighted by smoky torches and heated by open fires. There they feasted and drank and boasted of their adventures. Poets and singers recited the deeds of the great heroes of the past and told stories about Odin, Frigga, and the other Norse gods.

The Raids of the Northmen

In the time of Charlemagne, the Northmen began to give up their peaceful ways and to become a people of warriors. Charlemagne, you remember, conquered the Saxons of Germany and forced them to become Christians. At the same time, he tried to make Christians of some of the tribes of Northmen who lived not far from the Saxons. Charlemagne's methods were not gentle. When he conquered barbaric tribes, who were fiercely committed to their savage lifestyle—many of these tribes practiced child sacrifice and tortured their prisoners—he gave the people their choice of becoming Christians or of being killed, then and there. The Northmen were very angry at such treatment, and soon came to hate all Christians, especially the Franks. It was not long before these savage and brutal warriors began to strike back by making attacks on the Christian towns along the coasts of northern Gaul and the nearby island of Britain.

As long as Charlemagne lived, he was able to keep the Northmen from making many serious raids into his country. After his death, however, the Northmen grew bolder. Not only did they attack the seacoast towns, but also their long black ships made their way up the rivers and brought terror to the people who lived farther inland. No longer were the Northmen merely seeking revenge for Charlemagne's attacks on them. They had discovered that raiding towns was a much easier and more exciting way of making a living than by fishing and tilling their barren soil. The Northmen not only raided Gaul and Britain, but also sailed throughout the Mediterranean and attacked villages in countries like Spain and Italy. They had become a group of dangerous pirates who, as Charlemagne predicted, would never honor the life and property of others unless they were subdued by the sword or by baptism.

The Vikings liked raiding much better than trading.

Let us imagine that we are living in a seacoast town of Gaul in the days of the Northmen. Early one morning, as we lie sleeping in our beds, we suddenly awake to shouting outside. Rushing to the door, we find our neighbors gathering in a crowd and pointing toward the open sea. Dawn is just breaking, but clearly we can see long, low ships gliding toward the beach. Each boat has a single huge sail, and ten to twenty oars which beat in regular strokes as the vessel approaches. Near the carved monster's head at the front of each ship stands a group of grim, silent warriors in armor, their drawn swords in their hands, their shields held before their bodies.

As the first boat reaches shallow water, the warriors leap over the side and wade toward the land. Hastily the men of our village seize their swords and shields, and the women and children flee to the woods and fields in search of safety or foolishly try to hide in their houses.

The battle is short and bloody. Poorly prepared, our villagers are no match for the fierce warriors from the sea. One after another they are cut down, still trying vainly to protect their homes and loved ones. The Northmen rush into the houses and seize everything of value. The women and children are either put to death or rushed off to the boats as captives. As the attack dies down and the Northmen return to their boats laden with plunder, columns of smoke arise throughout the village. The houses and the village church have been set on fire and left to burn.

It is still early morning when the long ships put out to sea with their plunder and their captives, searching for another unprotected town along the coast. When they are safely out of sight, the few villagers who have escaped creep back and gaze sadly at the ruins of their homes and the bodies of loved ones. Nothing of value is left, not even the weapons and armor of the dead. No one will ever know the fate of the women and children who have been carried away. It is small wonder that the people of the seacoast towns prayed, "From the fury of the Northmen, O Lord, deliver us."

The Conquests of the Northmen

As time went on, the Northmen began to settle in the lands they raided. Soon they had established many towns in southern Britain, Ireland, and northern Gaul. A large band of Northmen under a leader named Rollo invaded the kingdom of the Franks. In order to make peace with them, the king of the Franks, Charles the Simple, gave them a large strip of land in northern Gaul. In return, Rollo and his people promised to become Christians and to be loyal to the king. The Franks' name for the Northmen was Normans, and Rollo's new lands became known as Normandy.

A group of Norsemen from Sweden, known as the Varangians, raided along the eastern shores of the Baltic Sea and eventually settled in Novgorod, Russia, and Kiev, Ukraine. Although the Northmen were cruel raiders, they were not cruel to the conquered peoples among whom they settled. Indeed, they sometimes adopted the speech, the customs, and the religion of their conquered subjects. The Northmen in Normandy, for example, adopted the language and customs of the Franks and soon developed a fine civilization very different from that of their relatives in the north.

Norse Explorations

We have already told how the Northmen learned to build sea-going ships and became a nation of sailors. During one of their early voyages they discovered the Faeroe Islands, far north of the British Isles, and used them as a stopping place for their fishing fleet. In 850, a Norse ship bound for the Faeroe Islands was driven out of its course by storms and came upon the coast of a large island still farther north. The Northmen named this new territory Iceland, though its climate was not much colder than that of their lands in northern Europe. Not long afterward, a Norse colony was founded in Iceland.

About a hundred years after Iceland was settled, a bold adventurer came to the island. His name was Eric the Red. He had sailed away from home because he had killed a man in his native village. After a brief stay in Iceland, Eric went aboard his ship and set sail for the west. He had a long and stormy voyage; but, at last, he came upon a land of rocks and snow and ice. Because he wished to found a colony there and wanted to make the new land sound attractive, Eric called it Greenland—a very poor name for such a place. Several shiploads of Norse colonists from Iceland went to Greenland with Eric and founded a colony there. It was not long before trade sprang up between the Norse lands in Europe and the colonies in Greenland and Iceland. Many people also believe that Eric the Red's son, Leif Ericson, visited the continent of North America and established a colony near Nova Scotia around A.D.1000. Although the records are not clear, a growing body of evidence is leading historians to acknowledge that the Vikings explored many parts of North America. Viking settlements have been uncovered in Newfoundland and Minnesota.

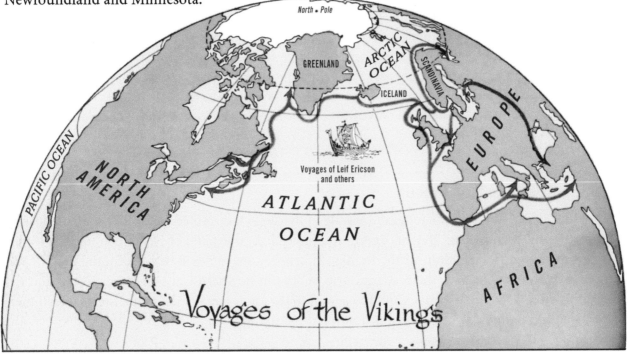

The Vikings from Scandinavia were among the first to sail across the Atlantic Ocean in an effort to establish colonies and find riches.

CHAPTER SUMMARY

The Northmen, or *Norsemen,* were tribes who lived in the lands where Norway, Sweden, and Denmark are now located. For hundreds of years the Northmen lived peacefully in their northern lands, hunting, fishing, and tilling the soil. At last they learned to build sea-going ships and became skilled and daring sailors.

When Charlemagne, king of the Franks, tried to subdue some of the more warlike and fierce tribes of Northmen and force them to become Christians, they refused to repent from their wicked ways and made raids on Christian towns along the seacoasts of Gaul and Britain.

The Northmen discovered how easy it was to make a living by raiding towns, and before long they developed into a nation of dangerous pirates, just as Charlemagne predicted. After Charlemagne died, an army of Northmen—led by a leader named Rollo—invaded the kingdom of the Franks. In order to make peace with the raiders, the king of the Franks gave Rollo a large strip of land in northern Gaul, which became known as Normandy. In return, Rollo and his people became Christians and promised to be loyal to the king, and stop their barbaric practices.

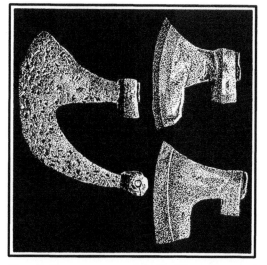

These battle axes were unearthed in Minnesota several years ago. Historian and author, H. R. Holand, visited 26 European museums to prove these finds were Scandinavian axes of the 14th century.

When Northmen conquered lands and settled there, they sometimes adopted the speech and customs of the conquered people. The Northmen in Normandy adopted the language and customs of the Franks and developed a civilization very different from that of their relatives in the north.

The Northmen made many explorations and discoveries throughout much of Europe, North Africa, and beyond. They discovered the Faeroe Islands and Iceland. Later, Eric the Red discovered Greenland and founded a colony there. Many historians believe that Eric the Red's son, Leif Ericson, also established at least one colony on the continent of North America, although there is growing evidence that the Vikings had settlements in several parts of North America.

At right is a translation of the inscription on the Kensington Stone, believed to have been left by Norse explorers in 1362 near the present site of Alexandria, Minnesota. Its lakes, not too far from the Great Lakes, would have been the practical means of travel for these early voyagers.

(We are) 8 Goths (Swedes) and 22 Norwegians on
(an) exploration journey from
Vinland through the Western regions.
(We) have 10 men by the sea to look after our ships 14 days-journey
from this island; year 1362.
We had (our) camp by two skerries
one days-journey north from this stone.
We were (out) and fished one day
When we returned home (we) found 10
    (of our) men red
with blood and dead. Ave Maria!
Save (us) from evil!

The only direct record of Norsemen in America. In 1898 a farmer near Kensington, Minnesota, found this stone engraved with runes. Scholars called it a forgery and for years it formed a step for the owner's granary. Then H. R. Holand translated it. Light hair among the Mandan Indians, North Dakota, suggests that Norsemen who escaped the massacre may have married natives.

CHAPTER QUESTIONS AND ACTIVITIES

1. Who were the Norse people?

2. Why did the Northmen become a nation of fishermen?

3. What were the ships of the Northmen like?

4. Tell about the life of the Northmen before they became raiders.

5. Why did the Northmen begin making raids on Christian towns?

6. Imagine that you lived in a seacoast town in the days of the Norse raiders. How would you feel about the Northmen?

7. Tell how the Northmen happened to settle in Normandy.

8. What sometimes happened when the Northmen settled among other peoples?

9. Name two lands discovered by the Northmen.

10. Who was Eric the Red? What did he do?

11. What continent did Leif Ericson explore around the year 1000?

KEY TERMS

Subdued   Faeroe Islands
Normandy   British Isles
Seize   Colony

Chapter 5

THE BRITONS AND THEIR CONQUERORS

O ff the western coast of the European mainland lies a group of islands called the British Isles. The largest of these islands is still known as Britain. Europe is one of the smallest continents, and the British Isles are only a very small part of Europe. Yet the people of these islands have played a very important part in the history of the world.

The Britons

About fifty years before the birth of Christ, when the great Roman general Julius Caesar was conquering Gaul, there lived in the southern part of the island of Britain a people known as the Britons. The Britons were savages, every bit as crude and uncultured as the early Viking peoples. Some of them dressed in the skins of animals, and some wore no clothes at all. They lived in small wooden huts in the forests and obtained food by hunting and fishing.

The Romans Conquer the Britons

After Caesar conquered Gaul, he led an army into Britain. Though his trained soldiers easily defeated the Britons, he did not stay, but returned with his army to Gaul. The next year, 54 B.C., he led his soldiers once more into Britain, but again he gave up the idea of conquering the island, and withdrew his army.

About one hundred years later, the Roman Emperor Claudius sent another army to the island. This time they conquered the Britons. Then, for three hundred and fifty years, the Romans ruled over the Britons. They divided the northern part of the island from the southern part by means of a great wall, named after the Roman Emperor Hadrian, to help keep out the savage Picts who lived in the north. They built stone bridges and stone buildings, which the Britons had not had before. Powerful Roman armies defended the Britons against all dangers. Under the rule of Rome, the Britons slowly gave up their savage ways

At its height, in the first century after Christ, the mighty Rome empire ruled over much of the civilized world. It established military outposts and political control wherever its armies conquered, even in the distant land of Britain.

and became a civilized people. After the year 300, Roman citizens and soldiers began to spread the teachings of Christianity to the people of Britain while they were stationed there or visiting. Many of the Britons eventually adopted the Christian faith as their own.

Then, suddenly, tribes of Goths attacked Rome, and the Roman armies in Britain were called back to Italy to defend their country. The Britons had no army of their own and they were left helpless. In addition, the Roman army never occupied or conquered the people who lived on the neighboring land of Hibernia, now called Ireland. Therefore, when the Roman army left the British Isles, raiders and pirates from Ireland began to raid the coastal towns of Britain with greater frequency.

Powerful Tribes Attack the Britons

Terrible times followed. One after another, savage neighboring tribes from the north and west swept down on the helpless Britons, burning their towns and taking their people as slaves. The worst of these raiders were the Picts and Scots. Even the Romans had never been able to overcome these fierce tribes from Scotland.

What were the Britons to do? On the mainland of Europe there were powerful tribes known as the Angles, the Saxons, and the Jutes. The unhappy Britons asked the Saxons to defend them against the Picts and Scots. The chiefs of the Saxons were very glad to do so; and, about the year A.D. 449, two Saxon leaders, Hengist and Horsa, landed in Britain with their followers and started to drive out the Picts and Scots.

The Saxon armies had good success in subduing the Scottish warriors and things looked promising. But when the Picts and Scots were driven off, the Saxons would not go home. They settled down in Britain and were joined by other Saxons and by tribes of Angles and Jutes.

This distressed the Britons, for they loved their country and were not willing to have tribes from across the sea settle on their land. They raised an army to drive out the Angles, the Saxons, and the Jutes and fought a fierce battle against them. Though Horsa, one of the Saxon leaders, was killed in the battle, the Britons were at last defeated. The Saxon leaders eventually determined to conquer the entire country.

These invading tribes pushed on, killing the people and laying waste the land. Buildings, homes, and Christian churches were burned to ashes. Here and there small bands of Britons, among them the famous King Arthur and his knights, continued to fight. Gradually, however, the Britons were completely overcome and driven from their lands. Some left Britain and settled on the mainland of Europe, but most of them fled to the west and hid in the mountains of Wales, leaving their country to the Angles, the Saxons, and the Jutes. Soon there were very few traces of the Roman civilization left in Britain. The country of the Britons was divided into several little kingdoms and became known as Angle-land. Later this name was shortened to England, and the people came to be known as the English.

For about 300 years, the Angles, Saxons, and Jutes often fought among themselves. They eventually established seven kingdoms—the Jutes formed Kent; the Angles created East Anglia, Mercia, and Northumbria; and the Saxons set up Wessex, Essex, and Sussex.

Christianity in the British Isles

During this time more and more of the people in Europe were becoming Christians. The Christian Church, with its leader the pope, was growing very powerful. But in Britain, the invasion of the Angles, the Saxons, and the Jutes had destroyed all traces of the Christian religion. Only the nearby country of Ireland remained a stronghold of independent Christianity, due in large measure to the work of the famous British missionary to Ireland known as Saint Patrick, who firmly established the Celtic Church by the time of his death in 461. About one hundred years after Patrick died, Columba and other Irish missionaries carried the Gospel to Scotland.

Now, in Rome there lived a monk named Gregory. One day Gregory saw some boys waiting in the marketplace to be sold as slaves. They had very light skin, beautiful faces, and blond hair. Never had Gregory seen such handsome boys. He asked where they came from.

"From the island of Britain," was the answer. "They are called Angles."

"They should be called angels, not Angles, for they have the faces of angels," said Gregory.

Gregory was very interested in these boys and felt badly when he learned that they were not Christians. He wanted to go to Britain, or England, as a missionary, to teach the Christian religion. Although he could not do so presently, he did not forget the boys.

A few years later, however, Gregory was made pope, and then he was able to send to Britain a worthy monk named Augustine, and forty other monks, in the year 597. They landed in the southern part of the island, in the little kingdom of Kent, and asked the king of Kent if they might teach the people to be Christians. The king was very kind and said that they might do so. He also allowed them to build a monastery in his capital, the town of Canterbury.

The famous missionary to Ireland named Patrick spent most of his teenage years as a slave in Ireland before his escape. In his early forties, Patrick returned to Ireland and, by God's grace, helped to set the Irish people free from the bondage of sin and idolatry.

In 597, an Italian monk named Augustine landed in Kent, England, with forty followers. Augustine preached to the King of the Jutes and he was baptized.

Augustine and his monks worked very hard. Soon they had taught the king of Kent to be a Christian, and most of the people of his kingdom followed his example. Other monasteries were built in other English kingdoms, and in time England became a Christian country. In time, thanks to the work of Patrick, Columba, Augustine, and other earnest missionaries, many of the people living in the British Isles became Christians.

Although the different kingdoms of England claimed to be Christian, they still fought among one another as to whether the church in the British Isles should be under the authority of the pope in Rome or independent, as was the case in Ireland and Scotland. The rivalry between the Celtic and Roman churches was finally settled in 644 at the Synod of Whitby, which decided the Church of England would follow the Church of Rome. The various kingdoms in England also fought over land boundaries and over petty issues of trade and economics.

The Danes

It seemed that England was never to enjoy a long period of peace. The Northmen, you remember, had begun making raids on the seacoast towns of Gaul and Britain during the reign of Charlemagne. The English called these Norse raiders the Danes because many of them came from Denmark.

In their voyages along the English coast, the Danes discovered that the towns were not well defended. Time and again they swept down on the coast, attacking towns, burning homes, stealing goods, and often killing both men and women. When a raid was over, they would quickly go away.

As time went on, however, the Danes grew bolder and bolder. At last they seized the whole country northeast of the Thames River and settled there. It seemed as though they might spread their power further and even conquer the whole of England.

Alfred the Great

In the year A.D. 871, a brave and able leader was crowned king of England. His name was King Alfred, the only English ruler who has ever been known as "the Great." He wanted to drive the Danes from the country so that he could unite England into one harmonious nation. Alfred was not content to merely rule over the portion of England known as Wessex, or West Saxony, for he desired to transform England from a collection of bickering kingdoms into one mighty nation under God. In the first year of his reign, King Alfred fought nine battles against the Danes. Sometimes he won and sometimes he lost, but even when things seemed darkest he would not give up.

There is a story, which shows us how patient King Alfred was in the face of great distress. After a fierce battle in which he and his army had been defeated, King Alfred was forced to flee from his enemies. He hid in the hut of a herdsman, who loved the king and wished to help him. The herdsman's wife, however, did not know who their visitor was and she was not much pleased at having another mouth to feed. One day, when she went away, she left some cakes baking by the fire and told King Alfred to watch them and not to let them burn.

The poor king was so busy thinking about his beaten army and planning more battles against the Danes that he forgot all about the cakes, and they were badly scorched. When the herdsman's wife returned and saw the ruined cakes she was very angry. She began to scold the careless guest bitterly. King Alfred patiently listened to all she had to say, and never told her that she was talking to her country's king.

King Alfred was also clever in outwitting his enemies. It is said that once he wanted very much to find out what the leaders of the Danes were planning to do. So he put on the clothes of a wandering minstrel and went to the camp of the enemy. They were pleased with his music and allowed him to stay, not knowing who he was because of the clothes he was wearing. While Alfred was there he overheard the plans that the Danes were making for a battle against his army. From what he learned he was able to defeat them.

In his early battles against the Danes, King Alfred found that when he and his men were defeated they were forced to flee for their lives. When the Danes lost a battle, on the other hand, they merely retreated to their ships and sailed safely away. As long as the Danes did this, there was little hope of really beating them. So King Alfred had his men build a navy of their own; and, with it, he succeeded in destroying many of the Danes' ships. From that time on, the war was much more of an even contest.

At last King Alfred defeated the army of the Danes, led by a mighty chieftain named Guthrum, and a treaty was made. By the terms of this treaty, the Danes were given the northeastern part of England that they had conquered. This land was called the Danelaw, and the Danes had to promise to stay there. Though the Danes often tried to break the treaty, Alfred had become strong enough to see that they did not succeed. Shortly after the war ended, the Danish leader Guthrum converted to Christianity and was baptized in the presence of King Alfred. As the years past by, many of the Vikings converted to the Christian faith.

The British Isles were under the control of various groups of people from different parts of Europe during its early history. Many battles were fought over a long period as these nations fought each other for control over Great Britain.

How King Alfred Helped the English People

King Alfred was a good scholar as well as a great warrior, but he was also a wise ruler. No sooner were the Danes defeated than he began to improve his kingdom in many ways and to unite his people into a strong, powerful nation. One of the first things he did was to rebuild the city of London, which had been partly destroyed during the war with the Danes. Alfred built finer and more beautiful buildings than London had ever seen before. He also put up a wall around the city to defend it from enemies and added large, swift ships to his small fleet to make it stronger. Because of this, King Alfred has rightly been called the "father of the English navy." Furthermore, he helped the workmen of his kingdom by bringing to England skillful workers from other lands. He did this to show the English how to carry on their own work as craftsmen and traders in a better way.

Alfred also set up a new code of laws for England that was based largely on the Ten Commandments and the Book of Exodus. As a Christian king, Alfred believed that only the Triune God of Scripture was both King of kings and the Supreme Lawgiver. Before Alfred's time, the laws in England were not very good. Each part of the kingdom had a different set of laws. What was forbidden in one part might not be forbidden in another. Alfred gathered all of the best laws into one book, which began with the Ten Commandments and ended with the Golden Rule. He required all the people in his kingdom, rich and poor alike, to obey these laws. When trouble arose between a noble and a poor man, the king always saw that the poor man was treated fairly and justly, as the Bible requires. This consistent rule of law helped to unite the Englishmen who were under Alfred's rule.

Throughout his kingdom, King Alfred had law courts established where everyone alike might have a fair trial. The people themselves carried on these trials, and they also elected officers called sheriffs to enforce the laws and keep the peace. Unlike most of the kings of his day, King Alfred allowed his subjects to have a voice in governing the country through a council known as the Witan. The Witan included many of the wise men of the kingdom, who helped the king rule by giving him good advice. As a wise and godly leader, Alfred understood that there is safety in a multitude of counselors.

King Alfred had great respect for learning, as well. Since he wanted to become as well educated as possible, he learned Latin and read the Latin books of the day. He built a library and had many of the most important Latin books rewritten in the language of the English people so that his subjects might read and enjoy them. Like Charlemagne, Alfred founded many church related schools. He also had a school in his palace for his children and the other children of the court. In the schools which he founded, the pupils were taught to read and write both their own language and Latin.

King Alfred was also an inventor. He invented a sort of clock made up of six candles, each of which would burn just four hours, making the twenty-four hours of the day. Each candle had two black stripes and two white stripes around it. Since it took almost exactly an hour for each candle to burn down through the width of a single stripe, King Alfred's candle clock was really quite accurate for telling time. He also invented a lantern with sides of such thin horn that light could pass through them. Before this time, the English had had only open oil lamps, which were forever blowing out in the wind; therefore, Alfred gave them the first practical lantern.

King Canute

For over one hundred years after King Alfred's death, England was ruled by kings who tried to carry on his ideas and unite the English into an even stronger people. At length, however, a Danish king, named Canute the Great, led an army from Denmark into En-

Church schools, and occasionally monasteries, taught young people how to read and write. Most youngsters during the Middle Ages had limited educational opportunities. Only the rich could afford to privately educate their children by way of tutors.

gland. Canute—known as Knud in Denmark—conquered England and became their king. He was a Christian, and a kind and just ruler.

There is a tale told about King Canute. One day, the king and the people of his court were near the sea. Certain courtiers, wishing to please Canute, told him that he was not only the master of the people of England but the lord of the land and sea, as well. He had only to command, and even the ocean tides would do his bidding. The tide was then coming in, so the king ordered his throne carried to the very edge of the water. Seating himself, he ordered the waters to stop rising. Of course, the ocean paid no attention to King Canute, and soon his feet were very wet indeed. Then the king turned to his embarrassed courtiers, who had flattered him, and scolded them for saying such a foolish thing. Canute exhorted, "Let all men know how empty and worthless is the power of kings. For there is none worthy of the name but God, whom heaven, earth, and sea obey." We can only hope that the humiliated courtiers learned a lesson that day regarding the fact that the earth and sea move at God's command alone.

In the year 1000, the Saxon King Aethelred tried to crush the Vikings who lived on the Isle of Man and on parts of the Danelaw. Of course, this enraged Canute's father Svein Forkbeard. Then in 1002, Aethelred married Emma, sister of Duke Richard of Normandy, hoping that this alliance would help protect him from the Danes. Feeling proud and secure, he ordered the massacre of all Danish men in England, including Canute's aunt and uncle. The next year, Svein came from Denmark to avenge their deaths, raiding the southern and eastern parts of England. The raids continued off and on for ten years. Then in 1013, Svein returned with his son Canute—this time to conquer England, which he did. Aethelred fled to Normandy. The following year, Svein died and Canute came to power; but Aethelred, seeing his chance to regain his kingdom, returned from Normandy and soon expelled Canute and his army.

In 1016, Canute returned and crushed the forces of Edmund "Ironside," Aethelred's eldest son and successor, at Ashingdown. Canute and Edmund signed the Treaty of Olney, which gave the Danelaw and the English Midlands to Canute while Edmund would retain control of the southern part of England. This was nearly the same thing that happened with Alfred the Great and the Vikings in the ninth century. Edmund died shortly after the treaty was made, so Canute became the first Viking king to rule the whole of England.

In 1018, Canute's brother—Harald, King of Denmark—died. So Canute returned to Denmark to take the throne. Two years later, he declared that Norway was part of his realm and eventually conquered that country, putting his son Svein to govern it. After that, Scotland came under the control of Denmark; and, by the late 1020s, Canute came to be King of all England, Denmark, Norway, and part of Sweden. He quickly united England by destroying *burghs*, or walled towns, that had been created to defend southern England from the Vikings of the Danelaw.

Canute's Accomplishments

When most people think of Canute, they recall the tale of him commanding the tide to halt; but he should be remembered for much more than that. He was the first king to effectively rule over all the Kingdom of England, bringing twenty years of peace within England itself and protecting it from outside attack. Because of this, Christianity, trade, and art flourished during his reign. Canute also respected the old English laws, to which he brought a keen sense of justice and a regard for individual rights. He was also generous to the English people, building many churches and giving gifts to others.

In 1035, Canute died at the age of forty. His sons, however, were not as wise or strong, and the Viking empire began to break up. None of Canute's children produced heirs, so one of Emma's sons by Aethelred—King Edward, the Confessor—came to the throne in A.D. 1042. He reigned for twenty-four years but proved to be a weak ruler. In 1066, he died, and his brother-in-law and chief adviser—Harold, Earl of Wessex—became king. But he was not to rule very long, as we will soon discover.

The Normans

The Normans, as you recall, were Northmen who had invaded Gaul, now called France. They settled in the region of northwestern France called Normandy, which lies along the English Channel. They had turned from their old religion and had become Christians. They had given up their old language for French. In fact, the only ways in which the Normans were different from the other people of France was that they were stronger, were more skillful in building and governing, and had a greater love for adventure and the sea.

William the Conqueror

When Harold was crowned king of England, a Norman ruler named Duke William decided that he would not acknowledge Harold's right to the throne. William wanted to be king of England, and when Edward the Confessor died, leaving no son, he saw his chance. He said that Edward the Confessor had promised him that he—not Harold—should be king and decided to fight for his rights. So in the year 1066, William gathered together his army and invaded England; this became known as the *Norman Conquest.*

The Normans, under the leadership of William the Conqueror, sailed across the English Channel in 1066 and defeated the English army.

The armies of William and Harold met near the town of Hastings. Harold's English army knew how to fight against the Danes, who fought on foot. The Normans, however, were fighters of a different kind. Many of them rode on horseback, and others were armed with long bows with which they could shoot deadly arrows fast and far.

Harold knew that if he attacked the Normans in the same bold way that he attacked the Danes he would be beaten. The Norman bowmen could easily shoot down his men while they were still at a distance; and the Norman horsemen could trample them to the ground, if they got close. So he drew up his men on top of a hill and had them hold their shields in such a way as to make a wall of shields around the entire hilltop.

The Normans came swarming up the hill but they could not break through the line of English shields. They were held back and the English spears and swords killed many. Seeing this, Duke William ordered his men to run away as though they were afraid. Many English soldiers followed them down the hill, and their shield wall was broken. Then the Normans turned, and the foolish English who had followed them were soon killed.

"I am still alive!" cried William the Conqueror to his retreating soldiers at the Battle of Hastings. He led his Norman army on to victory against the English.

Only Harold and a few of his men remained on the hilltop. They stood close together and fought fiercely. But the Norman bowmen stood at a distance and always aimed their arrows at the king. At last an arrow hit Harold in the eye, and he fell. The English then surrendered to the Normans.

William and his army marched to London, where he was crowned king of England on Christmas Day. Though his real title was William I of England, he is better known as William the Conqueror. Never since has an army from another country successfully invaded England.

The king had powerful nobles to serve him and help defend his kingdom. For these services he gave the nobles some of his land. The powerful nobles had lesser nobles serving them. The serfs served their local noble and obeyed his laws rather than those of the distant king.

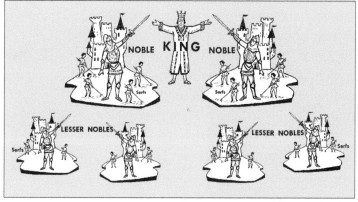

Feudalism

At the time William the Conqueror became the king of England, the English people had the same system of government that had spread throughout Europe after the break-up of Charlemagne's empire. This was known as *feudalism*, or the feudal system. Under this system, all of the land in a kingdom was supposed to belong to the king, who divided it among his nobles, or barons. The nobles paid no rent for the land; but in return for its use, they promised to support their king and to furnish him with a certain number of soldiers in time of war.

Each of the nobles had his own knights who fought for him. These knights wore heavy armor and rode on horseback. They were the strongest fighting men of their day. A noble also had workmen, called serfs, who tilled his soil. The serfs were not much more than slaves, though sometimes they had other serfs to work under them on their little patches of land. The people of each class were known as vassals of the class just above them, and had to serve them. The serfs and the knights had to serve the nobles and the nobles had to serve the king.

In the countries of Europe, this feudal system weakened the power of a king. If a noble fought against the king, his knights and serfs served him instead of the king. William the Conqueror was clever enough to see this danger and knew how to keep the kingdom under his control. He made all the serfs and knights promise to be loyal first to him and then to the noble on whose land they lived. He kept the strong nobles far apart so that they could not join together against him. He also taxed the people very heavily so that none of them could grow rich and powerful. The record of all their property was kept in a great book called the *Doomsday Book*.

What England Gained from the Normans

England gained much under the Normans, although some of the Normans' contributions were not good for the people. Being a quick-witted and skillful people, when they began a task they did it well. The many castles they built throughout the land were powerful and beautiful strongholds. Their cathedrals and monasteries helped to make the Church a great power in the land. They also brought to England many Norman customs and the French language, from which the English borrowed many words to add to their own speech. Weavers and other workmen came to England and started to work at their trades. This led in later years to the development of important manufacturing centers in many parts of England. The major problem of Norman influence stemmed from the fact that they moved England away from a de-centralized government, which included representatives from the people, to a centralized monarchy that placed the king above the laws of the land.

Serfs were forced to pay heavy dues or taxes to their feudal lord. The tax was often a portion of the food produced by the serf, but it could also be paid in coin. The local lord would often be under obligation to a mightier noble who would require his own portion of the tax as well as assistance in time of war. This fixed system hierarchy was the backbone of feudalism.

CHAPTER SUMMARY

The island of Britain was once the home of uncivilized people known as the Britons.

Julius Caesar twice took a Roman army into Britain and defeated the Britons in battle. Both times he went away, leaving the island unconquered. Later the Romans conquered the Britons and ruled them for three hundred and fifty years. Under the Roman rule the Britons became a civilized Christian people.

When the Goths invaded Rome, the Roman armies in Britain left the island and returned home. The Britons had no army of their own and were left defenseless. Soon ruthless sea raiders and invading tribes from Scotland and Ireland began to raid their towns.

The Britons asked the Saxons, a powerful tribe from the mainland of Europe, to protect them from the Picts and Scots. The Saxons drove away the invaders, but they themselves settled in Britain. There they were joined by other Saxons and by tribes of Angles and Jutes. The Britons fought against these invaders, but were finally conquered, and Roman civilization and the Christian religion almost disappeared from Britain. The country of the Britons became known as Angle-land, and later as England.

Saint Patrick, a British missionary who was independent from the Church of Rome, carried the Christian faith to Ireland, and he firmly established the Celtic Church, by the time of his death in 461. About a hundred years later, Columba and other Irish missionaries carried the Gospel to Scotland. In 596, one year before Columba died, Augustine and forty other Roman monks were sent to organize the Christian Church in Britain.

The Danes—Northmen from Denmark—made raids on English towns and captured part of the country. An English king named Alfred fought against the Danes and defeated them. Peace was secured and the Danes were given part of England called the Danelaw. Alfred was a good ruler and improved England in many ways because he was committed to placing God's Law over both nobles and common men and to work with his subjects through representatives.

After Alfred died in A.D. 899, the peace did not last long. A Danish army, which was led by King Canute, conquered England. Canute the Great was a Christian, and a kind and just ruler.

Edward the Confessor, the king who followed Canute on the English throne, proved to be a weak ruler. When he died, his chief adviser, Harold, Earl of Wessex, became king; but Duke William of Normandy also claimed the throne. William, therefore, led a Norman army into England, defeated Harold at the battle of Hastings, and was crowned king of England. He became known as William the Conqueror.

When England fell to William's guile,
it built its castles Norman style.

At the time William the Conqueror became king of England, the English were being ruled by the feudal system of governing. Under the feudal system, all the land in a country belonged to the king, who divided it among his nobles, or barons. In exchange for their lands, the nobles promised to support the king and to furnish him with soldiers in time of war. Their knights and their workmen, or serfs, served the nobles. Each person was known as a vassal of the person whom he served.

In order to keep the feudal system from weakening his power, William the Conqueror made all the serfs and knights promise to be loyal first to him and then to the noble on whose land they lived. He also kept the strong nobles far apart and taxed the people heavily so that they would not grow rich and powerful. These actions were inconsistent with a Christian king who should be preoccupied with urging his people to be loyal, first and always, to God and His Law.

England gained much under the Normans, although not all of the plans to centralize government power proved beneficial to the English. They taught the English how to develop and run a strong government with the king at its head. They also built many strong and beautiful castles and many cathedrals and monasteries throughout the land. They brought to England the Norman customs and the French language, from which the English borrowed many words. Weavers and other workmen came to England and started to work at their trades, which helped to expand the economy of England.

In the closing centuries of the Middle Ages, castles became very sophisticated and highly developed. This drawing depicts a castle in England during the Norman period.

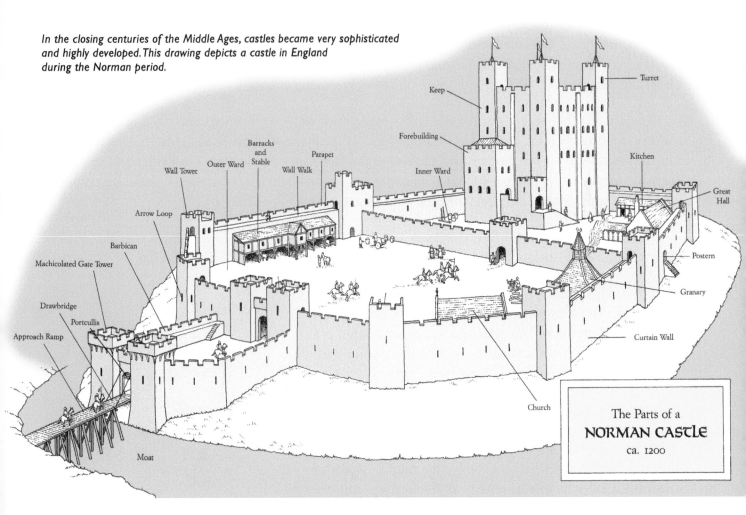

Turret

Keep

Forebuilding

Kitchen

Barracks and Stable

Outer Ward

Parapet

Wall Tower

Wall Walk

Inner Ward

Great Hall

Arrow Loop

Barbican

Postern

Machicolated Gate Tower

Granary

Drawbridge

Portcullis

Curtain Wall

Approach Ramp

Church

Moat

The Parts of a
NORMAN CASTLE
ca. 1200

CHAPTER QUESTIONS AND ACTIVITIES

1. What were the early Britons like?

2. Tell about the Roman conquest of Britain.

3. In what ways did the Romans help the Britons?

4. What happened when the Roman troops left Britain?

5. Why did the Saxons, Angles, and Jutes go to Britain? What did they do there?

6. Tell the story of Gregory and the Angles.

7. How did the Christian religion reach England after the invasion of the Saxons, the Angles, and the Jutes?

8. Who were the Danes? How did they happen to raid the English coast towns?

9. Tell the story of King Alfred and the cakes.

10. How did King Alfred learn about the war plans of the Danes?

11. What was the result of King Alfred's wars against the Danes?

12. In what ways did King Alfred improve England?

13. Tell about two of King Alfred's inventions.

14. Who was King Canute? How did he gain the throne of England?

15. Tell the story of King Canute and the sea.

16. Who were the Normans? How did they happen to invade England?

17. How did the Normans win the battle of Hastings?

18. What was the feudal system of government?

19. What negative effects did the Norman Conquest have on England?

KEY TERMS

Uncultured	Monk
Hibernia	Saxony
Augustine	Danelaw

Norman and Saxon warriors had interesting weapons.

Chapter 6
CASTLE LIFE IN THE MIDDLE AGES

Once there were hundreds of strong, beautiful castles throughout Europe. Even today some of them are still standing. Why were all these castles built? Who lived in them? What went on in and around these castles?

The Feudal System

After the break-up of Charlemagne's empire, there were no strong governments in Western Europe. All of the land in each country was supposed to belong to the king, who divided it among his nobles. In return for its use, the nobles promised to serve their king and be loyal to him. Each noble had *serfs*, or workmen, who lived on his land. Part of the land was set aside for the nobleman's own use, and part was allotted for the serfs' use. The serfs had to care for the nobleman's personal lands, as well as their own; and they also had to give him a large part of their own crops. No serf was allowed to leave his noble's lands without permission.

When a serf goes out to fish, he first must fill his noble's dish.

Many of the nobles were not powerful enough to protect themselves and their serfs from robbers or from stronger nobles. A weak noble would often go to a more powerful noble and—placing his hands between the hands of the more powerful noble—promise to give to him all his lands and to supply him with soldiers in time of war. In return, the stronger noble would promise to protect the weaker and let him continue to use his lands. The weaker noble was the *vassal* of the stronger, and the stronger was called his *lord*.

All throughout western Europe, weak nobles became the vassals of stronger ones, and the strong nobles in turn became the vassals of those still more powerful. In each country the most powerful nobles were the vassals of the king.

It was in this way that the feudal system gradually developed in Europe. In each country, the king was the lord whom the most powerful nobles served. Each nobleman, in turn, had vassals serving him, and sometimes these vassals had vassals of their own. Everyone in the country, from the king down to the lowest serf, had his place in the feudal system.

The Castles of the Middle Ages

In the days of the feudal system, most noblemen had a castle, and some noblemen had several of them. These castles were really fortresses. They had thick, lofty walls and strong towers. The entrance to a castle was usually a single gateway. The gates were made of thick, heavy wood; and an iron grating, or *portcullis*, could be let down close in front of them to keep out unwanted visitors.

Many of the castles were built on top of steep rocky crags or on mountaintops, where they could not easily be attacked. Other castles were built on islands or were surrounded by wide, deep *moats*, or ditches filled with water. The noblemen of the Middle Ages showed great cleverness in making their castles hard to capture.

In an effort to protect themselves from other nobles and lawless barbarian tribes, many rich nobles built strong fortresses called castles during the Middle Ages.

An Attack on a Castle

What happened when an enemy attacked a castle? Around the castle there was often a deep moat, which the attackers must first cross. In peaceful times, a drawbridge stretched from one bank of the moat to the other. But in battle, the bridge was drawn up against the castle wall, and the enemy had to find some other way to cross the ditch. With the arrows of the defenders whizzing about them, the attackers needed to build a bridge, fill up part of the moat with dirt and stones, or make rafts on which to cross the water.

When the attackers managed to get across the moat, they reached the outer walls of the castle. These walls were high and had openings at the top. Through these openings, the bowmen on the walls shot their arrows at the attackers. About every 200 feet along the wall was a tower, also pierced with slits for the bowmen. The towers stood several feet higher than the walls; and, from each one, a soldier watched the attack and gave orders.

It was not easy to force an entrance through the castle gates. The drawbridge lay flat against the outer wall of the castle, protecting the gateway. Behind it was the portcullis, which could be lowered so as to block the passage. The gates themselves were thick wooden doors set between two towers.

What could the attackers do? With great war machines they hurled rocks at the bowmen on the walls and tried to drive them from their places. Heavy logs, tipped with metal, were driven against the drawbridge and walls. These were battering rams. All the time, the defenders shot their arrows and dropped rocks and logs and even poured hot oil on the men below.

High ranking nobles and kings would often live in huge stone castles to protect themselves from enemies. Peasants and serfs would often live in small villages located nearby.

Finally, the attackers succeeded in smashing the drawbridge, forcing their way through the portcullis, and breaking open the gates. Then they would find themselves in the first courtyard. On three sides were the high outer walls, from which the bowmen still shot arrows at them. On the fourth side was another high wall or a line of sharpened stakes, called *pickets*, separating the first courtyard from a second, which lay beyond. All that the attackers found in the first courtyard were the stables of the owner of the castle, the chapel, and perhaps a few people from the neighboring villages who had taken shelter within the outer walls.

Breaking through the inner wall or the line of pickets, the attackers would make their way into the second courtyard. Here were the ovens for cooking and the storehouses for the food, as well as the buildings in which the nobleman and his family usually lived. Here, also, they found a stone building with thick walls and a very strong door, which was closed and barred. This is called the *keep*. It was here that the noble and his men made their last stand against the attackers. To capture the keep, the stout wooden door had to be shattered, and the armed and desperate defenders needed to be overcome as they battled to protect the passageways and narrow stone stairways, which led from floor to floor. When the keep was taken the castle would have been captured.

Castle Life in Times of Peace

The castles of the Middle Ages were much better fitted for war than for peace. The windows were too narrow to let in much light or fresh air, so the rooms were often dark, damp, and bad-smelling. They were often cold, too, for there were no stoves or furnaces, and the only heat came from open fireplaces. At night there was only the dim light of the fire and candles, oil lamps, or torches. Most castles had no glass in the windows, and very few had rugs on the floors. In most of the castles, the gray stone walls were bare and undecorated, but in some the walls were covered with tapestries, which were beautiful pictures made by weaving together colored threads.

Castles were often cold, damp, and gloomy places in which to live. The lord of the castle would often host a splendid feast in the Great Hall to cheer up his family and noble friends.

In spite of the few comforts, a nobleman of the Middle Ages led a pleasant and interesting life. He arose at the first light of day, prayed in the chapel, breakfasted, and set about his daily duties. While the women made the family clothes and directed the work of the servants, the nobleman and his sons mounted their horses and set out to look over their property. If the nobleman had much land, he might have one or more large houses, called manor houses, where the records of the nearby serfs were kept and where he and his family sometimes went to live when they grew tired of their dark and drafty castle. Each manor house had to be visited often so that the nobleman might see that the records of the serfs were properly kept. The nobleman and his sons also looked after the defenses of the castle and the weapons of their soldiers so that all would be ready for war on short notice.

Hunting was one of the most popular pleasures of the noblemen. It was also useful, for it supplied much of the meat for the castle. Sometimes the hunting was done with falcons, which were trained to kill ducks, pheasants, rabbits, and other small game for their masters. Many ladies had their own pet falcons and often joined the men in hunting. When wild boars, bears, and other large game were hunted, the women usually stayed at home, for such sport was dangerous.

Evenings in a castle were short, for everyone went to bed at about nine o'clock. After the heavy evening meal, the family usually gathered about the fireplace and talked or played chess, backgammon, or some other game popular at that time. From time to time, a wandering *minstrel*, or singer, was admitted to the castle and gladly entertained the nobleman and his family with songs and stories in return for a few coins, a meal, and a place to sleep.

Chivalry

As the feudal system developed in Europe, there grew up with it certain rules for the behavior of knights and noblemen. These rules did not have to be obeyed like ordinary laws, but every true knight and nobleman was expected to live up to them. The custom of following these rules was known as *chivalry*.

Chivalry greatly improved life in the Middle Ages. All knights and noblemen were pledged to respect women of noble birth and to help people in time of trouble. A knight or noble was supposed to be true to his word, and to fight fairly against his enemies. Even in that age of ignorance and bloodshed, many of the knights and noblemen lived up to the high standards of chivalry.

The son of a nobleman was carefully taught the rules of chivalry so that he would grow up to become a true and worthy knight. When he was seven years old, he left his mother and went to the castle of some great lord to begin his training for knighthood. There he was known as a *page*. He always attended his master and his mistress, waiting on them in the dining hall, following them in the hunt, and serving them in other ways. While he was a page he was taught to live a good life and always to honor and protect women. It was a knight's duty to be courteous, brave, and loyal, and these lessons the boy learned while he was still very young.

An armored knight's most urgent need—a mighty boost to mount his steed.

At the age of fourteen, the boy became a *squire.* He was then taught to ride a horse, to use weapons, and to hunt. For seven years he remained a squire. During this period he followed his lord in the hunt or battle, took care of his armor, and looked after his safety as best he could. All of this time the boy was growing stronger and more skillful.

At twenty-one, the squire became a *knight.* The evening before he was to be made a knight, other knights gave the young man solemn advice about what he must do. He was dressed in a simple white garment with long sleeves. He then went to the chapel, where he spent the night in prayer. The following day he was dressed in his armor. He knelt before the nobleman, who was to make him a knight, and promised to support and defend the Church and to protect the weak and helpless. Then the nobleman struck the young man lightly on the shoulder with the flat of a sword blade and pronounced him a knight.

Tournaments

Wars between the different nobles were very frequent in the Middle Ages, and the knights spent much of their time training for them. Contests, called *tournaments,* were held from time to time; and these gave the knights a chance to practice for war by fighting each other in a safer environment.

A nobleman proclaims a young man a knight with the words, "In the name of God I dub thee knight."

A king or a powerful nobleman usually gave a tournament at his own expense. Long before it was to be held, messengers were sent far and wide to spread the news so that all who cared to come might make ready. From every direction, people came flocking—noblemen and knights, merchants and minstrels, and sometimes even kings and princes. There were many ladies, too, who came to cheer their favorites. Stands were put up to seat the guests, and brightly colored tents and booths appeared everywhere. It was indeed a merry occasion.

On the day of the tournament, everyone gathered in the stands or stood against the fence which surrounded the field where the contests were to take place. At a signal, two knights rode forward, dressed from head to foot in their shining armor and holding their long blunt wooden lances upright. After saluting the lords and ladies in the stands, they rode to opposite ends of the field and faced each other. At the blast of a trumpet, the two knights leveled their lances, dug their spurs into their horses' sides, and rushed at each other. Each tried with all his strength and skill to knock his rival to the ground. This type of combat is called *jousting.* If neither was thrown from his horse, they tried again, and continued until one or both lay helpless on the ground. Sometimes the knights who fought were real enemies. In such cases, sharp lances were used, and the fighting went on until one or both of the knights were killed or too badly wounded to continue.

Wealthy nobles sponsored great festivals which featured colorful knights engaging in mock battles and mounted warriors jousting on horseback. Many of the knights were willing to risk serious injury in these so-called games in an effort to gain fame and valuable combat training.

After a number of these combats between pairs of knights, a contest between groups of knights commenced. The men taking part were divided into two equal forces. Each man was armed with a blunt wooden lance and a dull sword. At a given signal, the two groups charged each other from opposite ends of the field. As they came together with a splintering of lances and a clashing of armor, some men were sure to be thrown to the ground beneath the hoofs of the horses. Nevertheless, the contest continued. Those on the ground, who were able to get to their feet, drew their swords and fought against each other and against the men on horseback. Only when one group was beaten did the fighting stop.

These tournaments must have been very expensive to run and often costly for the participants in terms of broken bones or fractured skulls. The nobleman who gave the tournament had to feed the hundreds of people who came to it. Men and horses were killed or injured. Lances, swords, shields, and valuable suits of armor were ruined. Nevertheless, many tournaments were held throughout the Middle Ages, for it was thought that no knight could fight well in war unless he had first learned to give and to receive blows by taking part in tournaments.

Mounted knights were skillful fighters who had to train for years before they could be prepared for battle. It took great strength just to carry a heavy suit of mail, lance, sword, shield, and helmet. Can you identify these items?

The Serfs

There was a side to life under the feudal system which was much less pleasant than the carefree life of the noblemen and their families. In contrast to the nobles, the serfs who labored in the fields, indeed had few pleasures, and even fewer opportunities to better their standing in life.

Near each castle stood a little village where the serfs lived. The houses were tiny, dirty shacks, crowded close together along a single muddy street. Usually an entire family lived together in the same room, sleeping at night on piles of straw on the hard packed dirt floor. In the mud, before the doors of the huts, hogs lay and children played. The beautifully dressed lords and ladies from the castle must sometimes have shuddered as they passed by the dirty little village or saw the ragged figures of the workers toiling in the fields.

Every morning the serfs arose, ate what little food they had, and started out for their long day's work. Before they could even touch their own small strips of soil, the nobleman's land had to be tended. Part of everything they raised had to be turned over to the nobleman, and at times they also had to pay him taxes in money. The grain that they raised had to be ground at their own expense in the nobleman's mill, and their cloth had to be woven on his looms. If hunting parties from the castle rode through their fields and trampled their grain, the poor serfs could do nothing about it. If, on the other hand, a serf killed one of the

The home of the common serf was very crude with dirt floors and few windows. Poor living conditions often resulted in the spread of deadly diseases.

nobleman's deer or did something else that displeased him, the nobleman could have the serf locked in a dungeon in the castle, or whipped, or punished in some other way. If the land were sold, the serfs were sold with it, though the nobleman who bought the land could not send the serfs away from it. That was the only way in which the serfs were better off than slaves other than the fact that they were able to claim protection from their nobles during attack.

The peasants tried their best to entertain themselves with simple pleasures such as music and dancing.

Such was castle life in the Middle Ages. Around the towering castles and the manor houses with their jovial knights and lords and ladies lay the fields and villages of the serfs—miserable workers who toiled all day long to support the noblemen and their families. Is it any wonder why great and terrible plagues broke out commonly among the people who were forced to live in dirty huts and eat rotten food?

The Christian Faith Was Important to Common People

From day to day, the peasants had very little to do or to think about except hard work. Outside of a holiday now and then the Church was the only other interest in their dreary lives. Christianity had been the religion of these people for many years. It gave them peace of mind and an eternal hope in a society where there was still much warfare among the nobles. The Church did all in its power to put a stop to these wars, which always brought great suffering to the peasants. The peasants came to look upon the Church as their advocate and protector. From the teachings of the Church, the people learned to look for a life in Heaven, where all the troubles of life on earth would be forgotten. To the peasant, the solemn services, the beautiful stained-glass windows, and the sweet smells of incense must have seemed like a glimpse of Heaven. We must remember that in those days there were neither libraries, nor museums, nor theaters, nor motion pictures to which the peasant could go. Outside of his social times with his neighbors, the Church was the only part of his life that gave him happiness and a desire for better things than he had in his daily life.

CHAPTER SUMMARY

After the break-up of Charlemagne's empire, the feudal system developed in Europe. Most of the land was owned by nobles who had serfs, or workmen, who lived on their land and raised the crops. Lesser nobles who were unable to protect themselves and their serfs became the vassals of stronger nobles. That is, they served them in return for protection. The strong nobles in turn became the vassals of others still more powerful. In each country, the most powerful nobles were the vassals of the king.

In the days of the feudal system, the noblemen lived in castles, which were really fortresses in which they could defend themselves against enemies. The castles were not very comfortable to live in, but they were very hard to capture.

Noblemen, who had much land, had one or more manor houses where the records of their serfs were kept and where the noblemen and their families sometimes went to live.

The noblemen of the Middle Ages often lived pleasant and interesting lives. Their chief duty was overseeing the work of the serfs on their lands and making sure that the defenses of their castles, and their weapons, were kept in good condition. Hunting, playing games, and listening to the stories and songs of minstrels were common pleasures.

Chivalry was the custom of following the rules laid down for the behavior of knights and noblemen. The son of a nobleman was taught to respect women of noble birth, to help people in time of trouble, to be true to his word, to support and defend the Church, and to fight fairly against his enemies. Chivalry greatly improved life in the Middle Ages.

Tournaments were armed combats between knights. They were expensive and dangerous, but they were held throughout the Middle Ages in order to prepare the knights for real wars when they came.

The serfs lived in little villages near the castles of the noblemen. They had few pleasures and had to work very hard. They were only slightly better off than slaves.

During the last half of the Middle Ages, many small communities grew up and around the Church monastery compounds. The people who ran the monasteries sought to make them as self-sufficient as possible.

CHAPTER QUESTIONS AND ACTIVITIES

1. How did the feudal system grow up in Europe?

2. Imagine that you are a nobleman living in the Middle Ages. Describe what your castle is like.

3. What did an enemy have to do to capture a castle?

4. Describe the daily life of a nobleman and his family.

5. What were some of the pleasures of the noblemen?

6. What was chivalry?

7. How was a nobleman's son trained to be a knight?

8. Why were tournaments held in the Middle Ages?

9. Imagine that you have just seen a tournament. Tell about it.

10. What sort of life did the serfs lead?

11. Write down five specific freedoms that you enjoy that were denied to serfs.

12. Using an encyclopedia or the Internet, research the topic of the Social Security system's requirement to join this system prior to working in the United States. Pay particular attention to how the government denies people the right to earn a living unless they are registered with the Social Security system.

13. Compare and contrast the relationship that existed between a lord and his vassals with that of the federal government and workers in the United States under the Social Security system. Include in your answer a reference regarding the dues, or taxes, that are required under this system.

14. Why is it foolish to give up basic freedoms for protection or security?

KEY TERMS

Vassal	Moat
Serf	Manor
Noble	Chivalry

Chapter 7
THE CRUSADES AND THEIR RESULTS

For more than six hundred years after the fall of the Western Roman Empire, the nations of Western Europe were constantly fighting among themselves. Then suddenly, quarrels were laid aside, and thousands from England, France, Germany, and Italy traveled far from their homes to fight side by side against a common enemy. Where did they go? Whom did they fight? What cause was so important that it united the people of Western Europe?

The Pilgrims, the Arabs, and the Turks

During the first half of the Middle Ages (A.D. 500–1000), about which we have been reading, it was the custom of Christian people to travel to holy places to worship. People who made these journeys were known as pilgrims, and their journeys were called pilgrimages. Men and women usually made pilgrimages because they thought that God would be pleased and would forgive the sinful things they had done.

Most of the pilgrims did not travel beyond the borders of their own countries. They were usually content to go to some nearby shrine, or holy place, such as the tomb of a saint who was buried not too far away.

Some of the most religious pilgrims, however, wanted to go to even holier places than were to be found in their own countries. So they traveled hundreds of miles to Palestine, the Holy Land, where Christ had lived. Although the Bible states that Christ's death on the cross paid for all their sins, the priests told them that their greatest sins would only be forgiven if they could worship in the Holy City of Jerusalem. Since the pilgrims could not read the Bible in their own language, they believed the priests.

For a long time the pilgrims went to and from the Holy Land without danger from enemies other than hunger, sickness, and small bands of robbers. The Holy Land was in the hands of the Arabs, the people of Arabia, a country southeast of Palestine. Most of the Arabs were Muslims, or followers of Islam, but they often tolerated the Christians. They were willing to have the pilgrims visit the Holy Land and seldom bothered them.

East of the Caspian Sea, there lived a wild race called the Turks. In the year A.D. 1071, they swept down on the Holy Land and took Palestine and the Holy City of Jerusalem from the Arabs. Like the Arabs, the Turks were Muslims, who believed in the false teachings of Muhammad. Unlike the Arabs, however, they hated the bands of Christian pilgrims who traveled to their new land. They treated them cruelly, and many of the pilgrims were beaten and robbed and some were killed. In the years following the capture of Palestine by the Turks, it became more and more dangerous for Christians to go to the Holy Land.

The Council of Clermont

Something had to be done! The pope held a great meeting, or council, at Clermont, in France, and called upon the people to go and rescue the Holy Land from the Muslims—or Mohammedans, as they were called back then. What he said to the people so roused them that they shouted, "It is the will of God." From then on, these words, "It is the will of God," or "God wills it," became their war cry.

The Roman Catholic Pope urged many men to fight in the Crusades.

The First Crusade

A French monk named Peter the Hermit set out to gather an army to march against the Muslims. Peter was a small, dark man with a flowing white beard. He himself had been to the Holy Land and had been filled with horror at the cruel way in which the pilgrims were being treated. Bareheaded and barefooted, he rode on a mule from town to town throughout France and Germany. Everywhere he went, he told people about the poor Christians in the Holy Land and begged them to follow him there to help drive out the Turks. Soon he had thousands of followers.

All over Western Europe, people were gathering together in bands to march against the Turks. In the spring of 1096, several armies started southeast through Europe toward the Holy Land. They were called Crusaders, a name which comes from a Latin word meaning "cross." The cross, as you know, stands for the Christian Church, which teaches that the crown of eternal life and redemption is only obtained through faith in the work of Christ on the Cross of Calvary.

These first Crusaders knew nothing about fighting and had no supplies at all. Their leaders—Peter the Hermit and a poor knight named Walter the Penniless—had little control over them. Long before they reached Palestine, these Crusaders began to attack cities and to destroy the countries through which they passed. Fierce fighting followed, and thousands of Crusaders were killed along the way. Only a small part of the force that had started out reached the Holy Land, and the Turks easily defeated them.

A few months later, another army set out for the Holy Land. This group was made up of many princes, knights, and strong warriors.

They marched into Asia Minor and captured a number of cities from the Turks. Although their leaders were constantly quarreling, and hunger and sickness killed more Crusaders than the Turks did, they fought so well that they won battle after battle.

Peter the Hermit helped to launch the First Crusade.

One thing that happened will show how bravely these Crusaders fought in their historic cause. A small body of them had just succeeded in capturing the city of Antioch, when suddenly a large army of Turks attacked them. For several days, the Crusaders held the city against what seemed to be hopeless odds. Their supplies were all used up, and it seemed like there was nothing left to do but surrender. At this point, a priest who was with them had a dream in which God supposedly told him where to find the spear with which Christ had been wounded on the cross. The priest dug in the ground at the spot which the dream had showed him; and there, indeed, he found a spear. The Crusaders were sure that this was the very spear the priest had dreamed about; and they rejoiced, for they felt that they could not lose if they had such a holy weapon. Led by the priest with the spear, they rushed out of the city and fell upon the Turks. In spite of the odds, the Crusaders drove back their enemies by the very fury of their attack and won a glorious victory.

The Turks were splendid fighters, but they could not hold back the determined Christians. In the year 1099, the Crusaders captured the Holy City, put to death the Turkish soldiers who tried to defend the city against them, and established the Kingdom of Jerusalem. During the next few years, the Crusaders captured several other cities from the Turks and succeeded in bringing the Holy Land under Christian control.

For years after the Crusaders had taken Jerusalem, things went well and it looked as though the Holy Land would remain a Christian country. Though most of the Crusaders soon returned to their homes, some stayed and settled down. A government was set up, and the feudal system was established in Palestine exactly as it was in Europe.

Two military societies, the Knights of the Temple and the Knights of the Hospital, were founded to defend the Holy Land from the Turks, in case they should try to recapture it. The Turkish cities which had been seized were rebuilt and their walls and other defenses strengthened. Except for small and minor fights now and then, there was peace between the Christians and the Turks. Christian pilgrims once more began to visit Jerusalem in safety.

The Second Crusade

The thousands led by Peter the Hermit and Walter the Penniless, together with the army of princes, knights, and other warriors who captured Jerusalem, made up the First Crusade. The Second Crusade began about fifty years later. Except for one town, which the Turks had recaptured, the Holy Land was still in the hands of the Christians, but it was in great danger of being attacked by strong Turkish forces. The Christians in the Holy Land asked for help. Soon two bands of Crusaders set out, one led by King Louis of France and the other by King Conrad of Germany.

From the very beginning, the Second Crusade was unsuccessful. Unfaithful guides led Conrad's army many miles out of its way. Hunger and thirst killed thousands of his men. Bands of Turks followed the army, capturing stragglers and making sudden attacks on the troops. When at last Conrad reached the Holy Land, the greater part of his followers lay dead along the trail. Louis's army also had suffered from Turkish attacks and very few Crusaders were left. A halfhearted attempt was made to capture the strong Muslim city of Damascus, but the siege was soon given up. Louis and Conrad returned to their own countries without having accomplished anything.

The Italian port cities made money by moving Crusaders and their equipment to the Holy Land.

King Richard and the Third Crusade

After its capture from the Turks, the Holy Land remained in the hands of the Christians for eighty-eight years. Neither the Turks nor the Arabs nor any of the other Muslim peoples who lived around the eastern end of the Mediterranean Sea were strong enough to recapture it. In 1187, however, Saladin, the Sultan of Egypt, succeeded in uniting all of these different Muslim nations under his rule. Saladin was both a skillful general and a clever man. Gathering a vast army of Muslims, he swept through the Holy Land, quickly taking Jerusalem and almost all of the Christian strongholds.

When the news of Saladin's triumph reached Europe, plans were at once made for a third crusade. This crusade is known as the "Kings Crusade." Three rulers—King Richard the Lion-Hearted of England, Emperor Frederick Barbarossa of Germany, and King Philip Augustus of France—gathered their armies and prepared to march against the Muslims. Most of the German army never reached the Holy Land, for Frederick Barbarossa was drowned while trying to cross a river, and few of his soldiers were willing to go on without their leader. After many delays, however, the French and English forces at last reached Palestine.

The French were the first to arrive. When the English army reached the Holy Land they found the French already attacking the powerful city of Acre. The walls of the city were high and strong, and it seemed impossible to take it. But the Crusaders would not be stopped.

Day after day, the attack went on. Great war machines threw heavy rocks into the city, wrecking buildings and killing people. Battering rams crushed the walls to dust. The Crusaders were relentless. On every side rang their inspiring war cry, "It is the will of God." Mere men and walls could not stop such an army. The mighty stronghold of Acre fell.

Just when the conquest of the Holy Land seemed sure, Philip of France and King Richard quarreled. The French army returned to France, leaving the English to carry on the war alone. Without the help of the French, Richard knew that he could not take Jerusalem. Still, he stayed and continued to fight.

As the war went on, Richard and Saladin grew to respect each other very much. Each knew that the other was a great and worthy leader. At one time, Richard was sick with fever. Saladin, although he was Richard's enemy, sent him fresh fruits to help him gain strength, and snow from the mountains to cool his hot, dry lips.

Such friendly acts were better than any amount of bloodshed, for they led in the end to a peaceful agreement between these two leaders. This treaty allowed Christian pilgrims to go to and from Jerusalem without danger. But the Muslims still held the Holy Land in their power.

During the crusade, Richard had made many enemies, even among the Crusaders. On one occasion in particular, King Richard had offended Duke Leopold V of Austria. To avoid his enemies he decided to return to England secretly through Germany. On the way, he was recognized and taken prisoner in December 1192 by the Duke of Austria. For several weeks no one could find out where the king was being held. King Richard was eventually delivered to Emperor Henry VI who held him captive.

Legend states that Blondel, Richard's favorite court singer, wandered through Europe, singing at each castle a song which Richard himself had written. At last he was rewarded. When he had sung one verse, he heard Richard's well-known voice singing the second, and he knew he had found his king. Regardless of how true or false this story may be, we do know that the people of England eventually learned where their king was being held and what ransom they would have to pay for his freedom. After several months in prison, Richard was released in 1194 after a great sum of money was paid by the English people.

The Fourth Crusade

For about ten years after the Third Crusade, pilgrims continued to visit the Holy Land in safety. The pope and other church officers, however, felt very strongly that the Holy Land should be in Christian hands rather than under the control of the Muslims. So plans were made for a fourth crusade.

Men from throughout Europe traveled to the Middle East to fight in the Crusade to free the Holy Land from Muslim control.

The Fourth Crusade started with the best of preparations. A large army of knights—most of them from France, Germany, and Italy—gathered in the Italian city of Venice, intending to travel to the Holy Land by sea. At the last moment, however, their plans were changed by news from Constantinople, the capital of the Eastern Roman Empire. Word came to Venice that the emperor of the Eastern Roman Empire had been imprisoned by his brother, who was reigning in his place. The Crusaders agreed to stop at Constantinople on their way to the Holy Land and right this wrong.

In spite of the fact that Constantinople was a Christian city, the Crusaders laid siege to it and captured it. Once within the walls, they refused to obey their leaders. Buildings were robbed and then burned, and much valuable property was destroyed. Many of the people were killed when they tried to keep the Crusaders from entering their homes. It was unfortunate for everybody that the Crusaders agreed to go to Constantinople.

With the taking of Constantinople, most of the Crusaders lost interest in the real purpose of their journey. Many of the leaders took their knights and returned home. Only a small army went on to the Holy Land, and they were completely defeated by the first Muslim army they met. So the Fourth Crusade, for all its fine preparations, was a dismal failure.

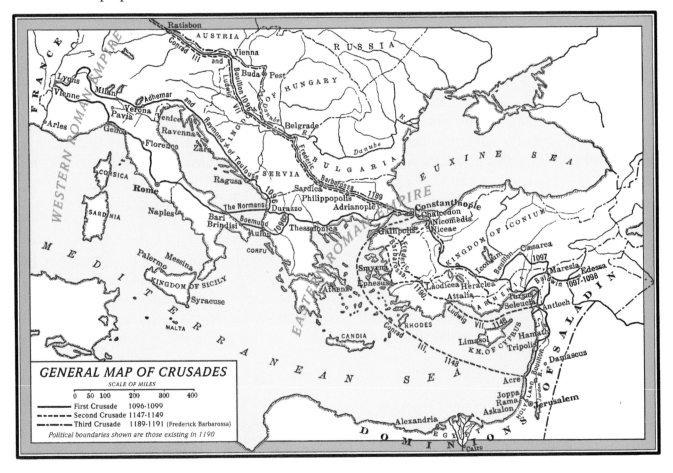

The Children's Crusade

After the Fourth Crusade, most of the kings and nobles of Europe gave no more thought to the Holy Land but turned again to managing affairs at home. Probably there would never have been another crusade had not the children of Europe suddenly become eager to free the Holy Land from the Muslims.

The Children's Crusade is one of the saddest things that ever happened. In France and Germany there were two young boys who really believed that the children of Europe could take the Holy Land away from the Muslims. So sure were they, that thousands of children joined them and started for Palestine, singing hymns and praying aloud. They apparently thought that God would protect and feed them and would roll back the waters of the Mediterranean Sea so that they could cross in safety.

Alas, no miracles occurred! Hundreds of the poor little Crusaders died along the way before the Mediterranean was even reached. At the seashore, many turned back toward their homes when they found no way of crossing to the Holy Land, but most of them died before they could again reach their families. Several hundred of the children were taken aboard ships by wicked men who promised to sail them straight to Palestine. It was not to the Holy Land but to Egypt that the vessels went, and the poor little travelers were sold as slaves far from their homes, with no hope of ever getting back. So ended the Children's Crusade, which was a sad testimony to what can happen when children forsake the rule of their fathers and presume to know God's will apart from the written revelation of God in Scripture.

Other Crusades

Shamed by the spirit of the crusading children, the kings and noblemen of Europe undertook several more crusades. None of them were very successful or very important. There was much fighting, and many Crusaders and Muslims gave their lives bravely. In 1229, the Crusaders once more gained control of part of the Holy Land, but fifteen years later they were forced to give it up. Palestine and Jerusalem remained in the hands of the Muslims from that time until General Allenby and a British army captured it in 1917, during the First World War. Certain areas of Palestine and Jerusalem are now under the control of the modern state of Israel, although some portions are still under Arab authority.

Effects of the Crusades

Though the crusades failed to rescue the Holy Land from the Muslims, they had many important results. In the East, the Crusaders saw rich rugs, beautiful brass bowls and vases, spices, and many other things unknown in their own countries. When they returned, they took some of these things with them and showed them to

When the Crusaders traveled through Muslim farmlands they were impressed by the skilled use of science and technology. Many of the best inventions of the East were brought back to Europe by the Crusaders and the merchants.

the people at home. These people, too, wanted some of these fine products for themselves. It was not long before traders were making regular trips to the East, taking with them some of the things made in Europe to trade for the eastern products. This trade, as you can see, was a direct result of the crusades.

The crusades also led many people to travel who otherwise might never have left their own countries. The tales which these travelers told when they returned aroused an interest in distant lands.

Ever since the fall of the Western Roman Empire, the Arabs and other peoples of the East had been the most learned nations in the world. Much of the knowledge of the Greeks, Romans, and other ancient peoples was forgotten in Western Europe after the Germanic invasions. The wise men of the East, however, had carefully preserved a great deal of the ancient learning by writing it in books. They had added to it certain important discoveries of their own in medicine, mathematics, and other studies. Now, as trade grew between the East and West, this knowledge began to spread throughout the nations of Europe and to help improve their civilizations.

The spiritual impact of the crusades is another effect that is often overlooked by modern historians. Although many of the crusades were poorly coordinated and planned, they raised the awareness of Christians in Europe to the suffering and persecution of thousands of Christians in North Africa and the Middle East. Many of these Christians were murdered or enslaved in the name of Islam. Sadly, only when a large number of pilgrims from Europe began to be harassed and some even killed, did the European leaders decide to launch a series of military campaigns to free the Holy Land from Muslim control. These campaigns raised the issue of the Christians' responsibility in protecting and defending themselves and other believers in foreign lands.

Perhaps the best lesson to be gained from the crusades, is that if government leaders are going to engage in a righteous military campaign against the enemies of religious liberty, they must plan and execute their efforts well. Christian leaders must count the cost before they go to war and then commit themselves to war only when they have the will to wage war in a Christ-honoring way. God-fearing governments in every age and time have the *duty* to protect and defend the liberties of their people to worship in peace and the *responsibility* to intervene on behalf of other defenseless people who are being systematically exterminated, such as Muslims were in Kosovo or Christians are in Sudan.

WHAT THE CRUSADES DID FOR LATER TIMES

The crusades aroused interest in distant lands, caused people to travel, and laid the foundation for widespread trade between Europe and the East. As a result of this trade, the learning of the East was spread throughout the nations of Europe, while the influence of European Christians was brought to the Arab race for both good and ill. The bloodshed between Muslim and Christian warriors established an enduring legacy of distrust and hatred between these two groups. Only the Gospel of Christ can bring true and lasting peace to the nations and break down the walls of hatred that exist between Christians and non-Christians everywhere.

CHAPTER SUMMARY

Long ago it was the custom of Christian people to make pilgrimages to holy places. Some even went to the Holy Land. When the savage Turks captured Palestine, pilgrimages to the Holy Land became dangerous. The Turks were Muslims, and did not like the Christian pilgrims.

The pope held a meeting at Clermont, France, and called upon his hearers to go and rescue the Holy Land from the Turks. Two large bands of Christians, known as Crusaders, set out for the Holy Land to drive out the Turks. The first group was poorly prepared and accomplished nothing. The second group—

made up of princes, knights, and strong warriors—captured Jerusalem and the Holy Land. These two expeditions made up the First Crusade.

The Second Crusade was led by King Louis of France and King Conrad of Germany. These Crusaders went to help the Christians in Palestine to hold the country against the Turks. Attacked by the Turks, many of these Crusaders were killed, and their expedition was a failure.

When a great Muslim leader named Saladin captured the Holy Land, Richard the Lion-Hearted of England, Frederick Barbarossa of Germany, and Philip Augustus of France, with their armies, started on the Third Crusade. Most of the Germans did not reach the Holy Land, but the French and English forces pushed on to Palestine. At first, these Crusaders were successful, but a quarrel arose between their leaders and the French army returned to Europe. Though Jerusalem and most of the Holy Land remained in Muslim hands, King Richard and Saladin made a treaty, which allowed Christian pilgrims to travel to Jerusalem in peace.

The Fourth Crusade was supposed to free the Holy Land from the Muslims, but instead the Crusaders attacked the Christian city of Constantinople. After the fall of Constantinople, most of the Crusaders returned home. The Muslims defeated the few who went on to the Holy Land.

In the Children's Crusade, thousands of children from France and Germany foolishly started for the Holy Land, only to die along the way or to be sold as slaves. Very few ever reached their homes again, for they had a zeal that was not according to knowledge, and God did not bless their efforts.

Several other crusades followed, but none were very successful or very important. Except for one brief period of fifteen years, the Holy Land remained in the hands of the Muslims until the twentieth century.

The crusades had many important results. They aroused interest in distant lands and caused people to travel. These military expeditions also led to trade between Europe and the East. As a result of this trade, the learning of the East was spread throughout the nations of Europe.

CHAPTER QUESTIONS AND ACTIVITIES

1. Why did the early Christians visit the Holy Land?

2. What happened to pilgrims in the Holy Land after the Turks captured it?

3. Why did the pope call a meeting at Clermont?

4. What was the purpose of the crusades?

5. Explain the first phase of the First Crusade led by Peter the Hermit and Walter the Penniless.

6. What did the crusade of princes and knights succeed in doing?

7. Tell the story of the Crusaders and the holy spear.

8. Who were the leaders of the Second Crusade? What happened to them and their armies?

9. What was the cause of the Third Crusade?

10. Tell about the Third Crusade.

11. What happened to Richard the Lion-Hearted on his way back to England?

12. Tell the story of the Children's Crusade.

13. What were the important effects of the crusades?

14. Draw a picture of a flag that would have been carried by one of the many armies that participated in the crusades. Research the topic of the flags used by Crusaders during the eleventh and fourteenth centuries to get ideas before you begin drawing.

KEY TERMS

Hermit	Arabs
Turks	Saladin
Muslims	Ransom

Chapter 8
TOWN LIFE IN THE MIDDLE AGES

Europe today is crowded with towns and cities. But in the early days of the Middle Ages there were very few. What caused towns and cities to spring up throughout Europe? What were they like? What did the people who lived in these towns do?

The Growth of Towns and Cities

In the early years of the feudal system, about A.D. 900, almost the only towns in Europe were the little villages of the serfs that stood near the castles of the noblemen. The noblemen controlled these villages.

Some of the villages were located on important highways, or near shallow places in the rivers where people came to cross. To these villages came traders, who brought with them rich tapestries, cloths, rugs, spices, and other goods from the Far East.

Early trade routes between Europe and the East.

As the serfs grew larger crops, fewer people were needed for farming. This left some of the serfs free to give their time to other things. As they wanted something to exchange for the goods that traders brought, some of them gave up farming and began to take up different kinds of work. Villages near forests soon became noted for the wooden goods their people made. Metal articles were made in the villages located near mines. In this way, manufacturing developed, and many of the villages grew into towns of size and importance. Stores were opened and shopkeepers sold goods to travelers and people of the town.

About the year 1096, at the time of the First Crusade, the people of some towns began to free themselves from the noblemen. They were not pleased to have someone outside their city make their laws.

Neither did they want to pay the high taxes which the noblemen demanded. As the towns grew larger, the townspeople learned to protect themselves against attacks, instead of taking shelter in their lords' castles. They built high, thick walls around their towns. Being independent in this way, they longed to break away entirely from the noblemen's rule.

There were several ways in which the towns won their freedom. Some towns actually fought against the nobles who were ruling them and, in that way, gained their independence. Many more, however, bought their freedom. In order to buy arms and armor and to pay his followers during a crusade, many noblemen needed much more money than they could easily raise. This money his townspeople were glad to supply on the condition that he give up his control over them. In his need for money, a noble often made promises of freedom, which he later regretted when he had returned from the Holy Land. But once the people had their freedom, they clung to it and would not give it up. In these and other ways, the noblemen—little by little—lost their control over the townspeople and the feudal system gradually died out.

During the Middle Ages, merchants had to use donkeys and carts to transport their goods and merchandise from town to town. As years past, merchants developed a series of overland trade routes that eventually became roads that lead from city to city and from country to country.

Peasants who worked the land were little better than slaves. These serfs were granted a small plot of land and a pledge of protection by their local lord. In exchange for this security, the peasant serf was bound to the land with little freedom and few pleasures.

The Towns and Cities of the Middle Ages

After they were free, many of the towns prospered. The money, which they no longer had to pay the noblemen, was now used to build better homes, finer shops, and stronger walls. In the later years of the Middle Ages, there were many thriving towns. Such cities as London, Paris, Venice, Genoa, and the Russian city of Novgorod became very important and were known throughout all of Europe. Rome, which had lost much of its importance after the fall of the Western Roman Empire, again became a leading center of civilization.

A Visit to a Town

Most of the towns and cities of Europe at this time were very similar, and a description of one will give us a picture of all of them. Let us pay a visit to a town of the Middle Ages.

As we approach the town we see first the high wall, which completely surrounds it. This is much like the wall of a castle. At the foot of the wall is a broad, deep moat like the moat around a castle. A wide drawbridge stretches across the moat and makes it easy for us to reach the gates. If, however, we were enemies, we would find the drawbridge pulled up, the heavy portcullis firmly in place, and the gates closed and bolted.

As we pass through the gates, we notice that the houses are crowded close together. They are constructed of wood and are five or six stories high, with steep, pointed roofs. On many of the houses the upper stories extend out several feet over the lower ones. The streets are so narrow that these upper stories almost meet overhead and shut out the sunlight and fresh air.

Most of the streets are muddy and unpaved, but a few are covered with cobblestones, over which horses clatter and the wooden-wheeled wagons rattle. There are no sewers, and the rainwater stands in the streets or flows in muddy streams along the wagon ruts. To our surprise, we see people throwing dishwater and scraps of food from their doors or windows into the street, with no thought of the mess they are making.

When we have carefully picked our way along the street for some distance we come to a large open square. This is the city center or marketplace. At one side of it stands a very beautiful building, the cathedral. The cathedral's towers reach high into the air and remind all visitors that the church is central to the life and culture of the entire town. For some time we stand looking in wonder at the beautifully made arches and the rich stained-glass windows. Many workmen are busy, and we find that the cathedral is not yet finished, though work on it has been going on steadily for more than two hundred years.

On the other side of the marketplace stands another large building, very different from the cathedral. It is square and made of stone and has a small and well-protected gateway. The windows are narrow slits. This building, we learn, is the citadel, the last refuge of the townspeople in case of attack. Even if the enemy succeeds in smashing their way through the walls of the town, they still have to capture the citadel before the town is theirs. So you see that the citadel served the same purpose as the keep of a castle.

Shops and Guilds

As we walk about the town, we see many shops but no large department stores like those in cities of the present day. We find that the shops of the shoemakers are grouped together on one street, the tailors' shops on another, and that each kind of business has its own section of town. Walking along the streets, we peer into many of the little shops. In one, we see men weaving rugs, tapestries, and cloth. In another, skilled artists are carving wood and ivory into beautiful and useful objects. We see a jeweler skillfully shaping silver and gold settings for precious jewels. These men have no large machines to help them. Each does his work by hand, with simple tools.

We enter the tiny shop of a shoemaker. All about us are pairs of shoes set in rows along the floor or on the workbenches. As we enter, the shoemaker himself greets us. In the back of the shop we see two young men seated on benches, cutting leather and preparing it for use in making shoes. The shoemaker tells us

that these young men are learning the trade and hope someday to be shoemakers themselves. They are called *apprentices.* There are no schools to teach them how to make shoes, so they have offered their services to the shoemaker, and work for him without pay, living in his house and being treated much as though they were his sons.

A Busy Day in a Craftsman's Town

The shoemaker tells us that these young men have been working for him for several years, and that soon they will no longer be apprentices. They will be given an examination in their work, and if they pass it and have money enough to start shops of their own, they will become *master workmen.* If they cannot afford shops of their own, they will continue to work for a master workman but will receive wages. Such paid workers are known as *journeymen.*

From the shoemaker, we learn that all of the industries of the Middle Ages are taught in the same way. The master workmen teach the apprentices and train them to become master workmen themselves.

The people in each line of business belong to a guild, or society, much like the labor unions or trade associations of today. The officers of the guild make rules regarding prices, wages, and the number of hours a man is to work each day, and see that these rules are carried out. They also give the examinations to apprentices when they feel that they are well enough trained to become master workmen.

Fairs

Most of the large towns have two or more fairs a year. Our friend the shoemaker tells us that his town is to hold a fair for a week beginning tomorrow, and he invites us to stay with him and visit the fair. This we are very glad to do.

As soon as his working day ends, the shoemaker and his apprentices lock up the shop and pass through a small door into another part of the same house, where they make their home. We follow them and are pleased to see that the shoemaker's wife is preparing dinner for us. The meal is simple but filling. There is no sugar and no pepper, though we are told that some of the wealthy people living in the nearby castle have sugar and also spices which a peddler brought from lands in the Far East to preserve their foods and make them taste better. The shoemaker's family uses honey to sweeten some of the foods, but most of the food is eaten without added flavoring. There are no forks, and we find that we are expected to use our fingers when eating. The water we drink has been carried in a wooden pail from a nearby village well. Soon after dinner, we go to bed on straw mattresses laid on the floor and pull thin woolen blankets over us.

The shoemaker wakes us an hour after daybreak, and we are soon eating our simple breakfast. Then we are off to the fair. In the marketplace, which we passed through the day before, we find a great crowd of people. Merchants have put up little wooden booths from which they sell their wares. Here we find peddlers and merchants from neighboring places as well as those from the town. Strange goods from many parts of Europe and even from the far-off lands of Asia to the east are offered for sale.

The fairs, we discover, are not only for the buying and selling of goods. There are amusements of many kinds. In one place we stop and watch a group of jugglers while they throw sharp swords high in the air and cleverly catch them by the handles as they come down. Some of the jugglers also balance poles on their noses or keep many balls in the air at one time. At another place we watch a man who has a large

brown bear that he has taught to dance. The man holds a chain, which is fastened around the bear's neck, and the bear walks slowly around on its hind legs, balancing first on one foot and then on the other. Singers and musicians are everywhere to amuse the crowd and to beg for coins.

By noon the crowd has become so large that we begin to realize that not all of the buyers could have come from the town. The shoemaker tells us that farmers from miles around have come in to buy goods and to be amused by the many entertainments.

Medieval fairs had thrilling sights, with dancing bears and armored knights.

Markets

Besides its fairs, each town has a market day every week. This is like a small fair. On visiting the marketplace on a market day, we do not find the many goods from distant lands which we noticed at the fair; nor do we see the jugglers and entertainers. The neighboring farmers and merchants are there, however, with their carts and their goods to sell, and almost all of the townspeople manage some time during the day to visit the marketplace and buy the articles they need. They can, of course, buy shoes, clothes, and the other articles sold by the storekeepers on any day during the week, but only on market day do they have a chance to buy what the farmers raise and the other goods not made in town.

The monks helped to preserve knowledge by copying important ancient books. Monasteries and church run universities also maintained large libraries that were available to scholars and theologians.

Universities

The next morning, we get ready to leave the town. Turning over the care of his shop to his apprentices, our host travels with us as far as the city gates. There we see four young men starting out on foot along the road. The shoemaker knows them, and calls them by name. We ask our host who the young men are and where they are going. He tells us that they are university students returning to their studies after a vacation. There is, he says, no university in his town, but there are a number of them scattered throughout Europe. One of the boys whom we saw leaving the town is going to study religion at the University of Paris, one of the oldest universities in the world. Another is going to the University of Salerno, in Italy, to study medicine so he can become a doctor and heal the sick. A third is going to the Italian University of Bologna to study law. The fourth is going to the University of Prague in Bohemia—a medieval German state, now part of the Czech Republic—to learn languages and art. Some other boys from the town have already left to take up their studies at the famous universities of Oxford and Cambridge in England, and Heidelberg in Germany.

Since we seem interested, our friend the shoemaker tells us more about the European universities of that day. We learn that their students come from many parts of the world, and usually they continue to wear the clothing of their native countries. There are no girls in the universities, for women are trained in the art of homemaking; not business, law, or theology. Most of the students wear swords or daggers; and sword fights, or *duels*, are common. The classes are held in small rooms, each professor having only a few students at a time. The shoemaker says that he has heard that the boys are receiving a splendid education at their different universities, and he is sure that they are also having a good time, as life is very interesting in the big cities.

We are sorry to leave the little town of the Middle Ages and our kind host the shoemaker, but at last we start off. As we reach a bend in the road, we turn for a last look at the wall and gates of the friendly town we have visited.

Chapter Summary

In the early years of the feudal system, about A.D. 900, almost the only towns in Europe were the little villages of the serfs, which stood near the castles of the noblemen.

As trade grew up, many of the serfs gave up being farmers and began to make and sell different articles. Some of the little villages grew into towns.

About the year 1096, at the time of the First Crusade, a number of the towns began to free themselves from the noblemen who owned them. After they were free, many of the towns of the Middle Ages prospered. London, Paris, Genoa, Venice, and Novgorod were among the leading cities, and Rome once more became important.

The cities and towns of the Middle Ages were usually surrounded by walls and protected by moats. Drawbridges, heavy gates, and portcullises helped to keep the enemy out of a city in case of attack.

The houses in the towns of the Middle Ages were made of wood and were crowded close together. Often the upper stories extended out over the streets. The streets were mostly unpaved and there were no sewers to carry off rainwater. Dishwater and scraps of food were dumped in the streets and left there to rot where they often spread germs or disease.

A town of the Middle Ages usually had a large open square known as the city center or marketplace. In the center of town was the cathedral, which symbolized the centrality of the church, and also the citadel—the last refuge of the townspeople in case of attack.

There were many small shops but no large department stores. Shops of the same kind were grouped together on the same street. The shopkeepers had their homes in the same buildings as their shops.

During the Middle Ages there were no schools to teach trades. Boys who wished to learn a trade worked for a master workman without pay for several years. During this time, they were known as apprentices. When they had learned their trade, the apprentices were given an examination; and, if their work was good enough, they were allowed to set up shops of their own. If they did not have money enough to set up their own shops, they continued to work for master workmen. They were then called journeymen and received wages for their work.

The people in each line of work belonged to a guild, or society. The officers of these guilds made and enforced rules that governed all of their workmen.

Each town held two or more fairs a year. Merchants came from far and near to sell their goods, and there were many entertainers. All of the townspeople and farmers for miles around came to buy goods or to be amused.

Once every week, each town had a market day when nearby merchants and farmers brought their goods to be sold in the marketplace.

Many universities were started in Europe during the Middle Ages. Among the important ones were the University of Paris, the University of Salerno, the University of Bologna, the University of Prague, Oxford University, Cambridge University, and the University of Heidelberg. Students came to these universities from many countries.

CHAPTER QUESTIONS AND ACTIVITIES

1. When did towns and cities begin to spring up in Europe? Why did some of them become important?
2. How did the towns of the Middle Ages free themselves from the noblemen?
3. Name several important cities of the Middle Ages.
4. How were the towns of the Middle Ages protected?
5. In what kind of houses did the townspeople of the Middle Ages live?
6. Why did towns often have a citadel?
7. Why were churches or cathedrals normally built in the center of town?
8. Describe the shops of the Middle Ages.
9. Imagine that you are a master workman. How did you learn your trade?
10. Of what use were the guilds?
11. Imagine that you have visited a fair of the Middle Ages. Tell about it.
12. What happened once a week in the marketplace?
13. Name two universities in Europe during the Middle Ages.

KEY TERMS

Tapestries	Guild
Citadel	Merchant
Apprentice	Journeymen

Chapter 9
THE RIGHTS OF ENGLISHMEN

At the time of the First Crusade, the common people of England had almost no rights or privileges. But soon after the last crusade, Englishmen were enjoying more rights and privileges than the people of any other nation. What were these "rights of Englishmen," and why did the English kings grant them to the people?

The English Barons

William the Conqueror, the first Norman king of England, was a strong and just ruler, but the kings who followed William were weak. They could not control the barons, or noblemen, who became very powerful. Without the king's permission, many of them built strong castles in which they could defend themselves against each other and even against the king himself.

Each baron was the ruler of the lands near his castle. This powerful ruler was often cruel to the people living on his land.

Only wealthy knights could afford a suit of armor. Each suit was custom made and was, in many respects, a work of art. The development of gun powder and accurate artillery forced knights to abandon personal armor except for ceremonial occasions.

He made them do whatever he wished; and, if they did something that he did not like, he punished them or even had them put to death. Of course, none of the barons had a right to do such things, but the barons were strong and the kings were too weak to protect the people. During this time the common people of England had almost no rights and they were very miserable.

King Henry the Second

In 1154, a strong king, named Henry II, came to the throne of England. He saw how miserable his people were, and he attempted to help them. He told the barons that they must tear down the strong castles they had built without permission. When some of them refused, he led a powerful army against them and made them obey his command. At the same time, King Henry made it very plain that he, and not the barons, would rule over the people.

Trial by Jury

Perhaps the most valuable thing that King Henry did for the people of England was to improve the courts and the ways of trying law cases. Before his time, a single judge tried most cases and decided by himself whether the accused person was guilty or innocent and what the punishment should be. Many of these judges were noblemen who had taken for themselves the right of trying and punishing the people who lived on their lands. Too often the judges used their great power unfairly.

One of the ways in which a judge sometimes decided whether a person was guilty or innocent was to try him "by ordeal." The accused person was forced to hold a piece of hot iron in his hand or to thrust his hand into boiling water. If his wounds healed quickly it was thought that God had proved his innocence, and he was not punished. If his wounds did not heal quickly, he was considered guilty.

Cases between two men were often settled by "trial by combat," or battle. Each was armed and made to fight the other. The man who won the fight was the winner of the trial, for it was believed that God would give victory only to the one who was in the right.

King Henry took the power away from the judges who held the trials. In their place, he appointed judges who were responsible to him for the fairness of their decisions. The king's judges traveled from town to town throughout the kingdom. When one of the judges reached a town, a body of men, known as the *grand jury*, gave him the names of all of the people who were to be tried. Each of these cases had been carefully considered by the grand jury, so that only those who deserved it were brought to trial. The king's judge, who was known as the local *magistrate*, then heard and decided these cases.

Twelve good men, all tried and true, made England's jury something new.

In later years, the plan of trial, which King Henry had started, was carried still further. Another body of men, known as the *petty* (or *petit*) *jury*, judged the people named by the grand jury. The petty jury listened carefully to the stories of all witnesses; then they considered what they had heard and decided whether or not the accused person was guilty. If the prisoner was found guilty, the judge then said what the punishment should be. Under this plan of trial by jury, Englishmen were sure, for the first time, of having a fair trial.

King Richard the First

King Henry II was followed by his son, Richard I, also called Richard the Lion-Hearted. King Richard, as you know, was a great fighter and a famous Crusader. Most of his reign, however, was spent away from England and he did little to help the people of his kingdom.

A few years after Richard the Lion-Hearted returned from the Third Crusade, he was killed by an arrow while attacking a castle in France. His brother John then became king of England.

King John

John was one of the worst kings that England ever had. He was lazy and cruel and cared for nothing but his own pleasures. Shortly after he was crowned, he began to realize that his people did not like him. He feared that they would drive him from the throne and make his little nephew, Prince Arthur, king in his place. So King John had poor little Arthur locked up in a tower. It is said that the king sent a man to burn out the little prince's eyes with hot irons. The man whom the king sent was used to doing cruel things; but, when he saw how small Prince Arthur was and how he trembled and sobbed with fright, the man's heart was touched and he went away without harming the little boy. Nevertheless, King John sent other men, who, it is believed, put Prince Arthur to death.

There is a story that shows the unfair way in which John ruled his people. After he fought a war with France and lost all of his French lands, he announced that he would try to get them back. He gathered together a large army and many ships for another war against France. When all of the soldiers and sailors had left their homes and work, John changed his mind and said that there would be no war after all. But he made the soldiers and sailors pay him money before going home, because he had not made them go to war.

John also quarreled with the pope at Rome. The pope had appointed a man named Stephen Langton as archbishop of Canterbury, a high office in the Church. King John consistently refused to recognize him as the archbishop. In order to punish the king, the pope forbade all church services throughout England except the baptism of babies and the service for those who were dying. This was, obviously, not right to do before God and was a terrible thing. It frightened the English people so much that John was at last forced to give in. Stephen Langton became archbishop, and the king had to admit that he was wrong and pay a large sum of money to the pope at Rome.

A famous English legend tells of a bold leader named Robin Hood, who lived during the reign of King John. Robin Hood and his men hated to see the poor people of England being mistreated by the king and his officers. Whenever they could, they righted the wrongs which had been done. The king's men soon came to fear Robin Hood, and the poor people learned to love him. Even if the stories about Robin Hood are not true, the people who lived in King John's time must have longed for a leader like Robin Hood who would free them from the king's injustice and protect them from his cruelty.

The Magna Carta

It seems strange that King John's cruel and heartless reign could lead to more good than harm. But that is what happened in the mysterious providence of God. The more unjust his laws became, the more discontented the barons of England grew. At last they decided that they would no longer put up with the king's way of doing things.

Gathering an army, they marched to London and told the king he must do as they asked or they would fight. They said he must sign a statement giving back to the people the rights which he had taken from them, as well as promising them certain other rights which they had not had before.

What could the king do when all his people hated him? Much against his will, on June 15, 1215, John signed the statement, which is called the *Magna Carta*, or Great Charter.

English Common Law originated from the rights of English people that were set forth in the Magna Carta, or Great Charter.

This signing of the Great Charter was a splendid victory for the English people. Among other things, it put an end to the king's power to throw a man in prison and keep him there, perhaps for years, without giving him a chance to prove his innocence. The Charter said that every man who was arrested must be tried in court; and, if it were not proved that he had done wrong, he must be set free. Also, according to the Charter, the king could no longer make the people pay him money unless he first got the consent of a body of nobles and bishops known as the Great Council. Like the Witan of King Alfred's day, the Great Council was to advise the king and help him in governing the country. One of the most helpful rules enacted by the Council led to the establishment of a system of standardized weights and measures for English goods. The Council was also responsible for seeing that the king kept the promises made in the Great Charter.

Although King John signed the Charter, he did not mean to give the people the rights it promised them. He hired troops to fight for him and attacked the barons. But before he could overcome them, he became sick and died. Though many changes have since been made in the terms of the Great Charter, it stands today as part of the English law.

King Henry the Third and Simon de Montfort

King John's son, Henry III, came to the throne after his father's death. He was almost as bad a king as his father had been. In spite of the Great Charter, he insisted on taxing the people heavily without the consent of the Great Council. The barons would not agree to this.

Led by a nobleman named Simon de Montfort, they made war upon King Henry and took him prisoner. For a time after that, England was ruled by a group of noblemen headed by Simon de Montfort.

Parliament

Simon de Montfort changed the Great Council and made it the first English Parliament. Two men from each of the leading towns and cities and two from each county were added to the nobles and bishops who made up the Council. This meant that, for the first time, the common people were to have a voice in the government through representatives.

In the same year that Parliament was formed, Henry's son Edward decided to get back the throne. Gathering an army of barons who had become jealous of Simon de Montfort's power, Edward attacked de Montfort. In the battle that followed, de Montfort was killed. Henry III once more ruled England, but now he dared not rule in the same cruel way he had before.

King Edward the First

King Henry's son, Edward I, was a strong, ruthless, yet clever king. Early in his reign he led his army into Wales and Scotland, conquering both countries and making them part of his kingdom. Soon after conquering Wales, King Edward visited the Welsh people and made a speech before them. In his arms he held a little baby, Prince Edward, his oldest son. Prince Edward, he declared, was to be the Prince of Wales and when he grew up he was to see that the people of that country continued to submit to his tyrannical rule. To this day the English king's oldest son is known as the Prince of Wales, even though the authority granted to such modern monarchs is minimal.

King Edward did manage to change and improve the English Parliament. In place of a single body, he divided it into two parts, or houses. One of these, the House of Lords, was made up of noblemen and church officials. The other part, the House of Commons, was made up of men chosen by the common people. King Edward's new Parliament is known as the "Model Parliament," because it has served as the model for all later Parliaments.

Even today the English Parliament is not very different from King Edward's "Model Parliament." The House of Lords and the House of Commons still exist. But, little by little, the House of Commons has gained power. In the old days, the king had much power in governing, and the House of Lords was more important than the House of Commons. Today the House of Commons has more power than the House of Lords and the king has almost no power at all. England may truly be said to be governed by the English people through elected representatives.

RIGHTS WHICH HAVE COME TO US FROM THE ENGLISH PEOPLE

- The right of a fair trial by jury.
- The right of having a voice in the running of the government and in fixing taxes.
- The right to have a just and uniform standard of weights and measures for money and goods.

CHAPTER SUMMARY

After the death of William the Conqueror, the barons of England became very powerful. They treated the common people badly.

King Henry II took away the power of the barons and made them stop abusing the common people. He also improved the courts and the ways of trying law cases, so that people accused of crimes were tried more fairly than they had been before.

King Richard the Lion-Hearted was a great fighter and a famous Crusader, but he spent most of his time away from England and did little to help his people.

King John was a wicked and selfish king. He did many cruel and unfair things. The barons of England arose against King John and made him sign the *Magna Carta*, or Great Charter, promising the people many rights that they had not had before. The king did not want to keep the promises which he had made in the Great Charter. He hired troops to help him overcome the barons but died before the war ended.

King Henry III tried to break the promises in the Great Charter. The barons eventually overthrew him. For a time the government was run by a group of nobles with Simon de Montfort at the head. Simon de Montfort formed the first English Parliament, made up of nobles, bishops, and men chosen from the common people. King Henry's son, Edward I, overcame Simon de Montfort and won back the throne for his father.

King Edward I ruthlessly conquered Wales and Scotland and forced them to serve his kingdom. He also improved the English Parliament by dividing it into two bodies, the House of Lords and the House of Commons. King Edward's Parliament was called the "Model Parliament."

Even today the English Parliament is much like King Edward's "Model Parliament." Now the House of Commons is the most important branch, and the English people may truly be said to run their own government through elected representatives.

CHAPTER QUESTIONS AND ACTIVITIES

1. How did the English barons treat the common people after the death of William the Conqueror?

2. In what two ways did King Henry II help his people?

3. Tell about the early ways of judging whether a person was guilty or innocent of a crime.

4. What was the method of judging which King Henry II started?

5. For what is King Richard I noted?

6. Tell the story of Prince Arthur.

7. What unjust thing did King John do to his soldiers and sailors?

8. Tell about King John's quarrel with the pope.

9. How did the barons get King John to sign the *Magna Carta*?

10. Name some of the rights that the *Magna Carta* gave the English people.

11. What finally happened to King John?

12. Why did the English barons go to war against King Henry III?

13. How did Simon de Montfort change the Great Council? What was it then called?

14. How did King Edward I add Scotland and Wales to his kingdom?

15. Tell about King Edward I and his "Model Parliament."

KEY TERMS

Baron	Archbishop
Nobleman	Great Charter
Magistrate	Parliament

Chapter 10
THE AWAKENING IN EUROPE

In your study of the Middle Ages, you have come to the period when many great changes were taking place in Europe. To understand what was happening, you will need to consider facts you have gained in studying the crusades, the rise of separate European nations, and the feudal system.

The Awakening

As the early Middle Ages—or Dark Ages—drew to a close, a new era in European history was beginning to dawn. This period of renewed interest in education and culture is called the *Renaissance*. The word means "a time of awakening or new birth." It was a time of hard work and enthusiasm in art, literature, and science. Some men studied the civilizations of Greece and Rome. For better and for worse, they were inspired by the fallible but interesting ideas of Greek and Roman thinkers and artists. Eventually, God used the Renaissance to lead great numbers of people in Europe to explore the greatest study of all—the study of God and His relationship with man. It was not until the unfolding of the Protestant Reformation, however, that learned men would begin to develop a truly positive and comprehensive worldview. We will learn about the wonderful period of Reformation that followed on the heels of the Renaissance in the next chapter.

The Dark Ages

Many changes and events sparked the beginning of the Renaissance. As you have seen, Western Europe was not very interested in books, education, or the arts during the Dark Ages. Monks and independent missionaries kept some learning alive in monastery and convent schools. Merchants started a few schools in which boys learned writing and mathematics. Certain training was also given to young pages and squires in preparing them for knighthood. Nevertheless, during the Dark Ages many people were kept in spiritual and political bondage due to their ignorance and pagan superstitions. They were too busy making a living, fighting barbarians, or being barbarian conquerors, to think much about education, religion, and individual responsibility. Worldly-minded churchmen and others in authority told men and women what to think and do, and they often withheld the light of truth from needy people.

Universities Are Founded

The earliest European universities were established at monastery schools. After the crusades, universities appeared in many parts of Europe. Boys and men, young and old alike, flocked to them. There were few scrolls or textbooks. Students searched monasteries for old manuscripts. Some were able to obtain biblical manuscripts and old Greek and Roman writings that had been copied and preserved by Christian societies in Ireland and Scotland. Over time, however, many university scholars became more and more influenced by pagan Greek or Roman philosophers and desired to do more than study religion, law, and medicine. As a consequence, university programs were broadened to include many subjects, some of which promoted the false idea that man could gain, by his own independent effort, all necessary understanding, without reference to the wisdom of God's written revelation—the Bible. It would not be until the Reformation era that scholars could begin to understand how biblical truth would inform and enrich the study of science and spawn technology.

Effects of the Crusades

You have seen that the crusades had an important part in changing the thinking and habits of Western Europeans. On their journeys to and from the Holy Land, Crusaders went through many countries. They met many new people and were exposed to teachers, scientists, and inventors from the Middle East. They were amazed at the education, culture, and wealth they found in Byzantium—also known as Constantinople. Here they first met scholars who spoke Greek and who could read the Greek manuscripts kept in Byzantine libraries.

Ancient manuscripts were made with great care and diligence. In many respects, these books were beautifully illustrated works of art.

When they reached Palestine, the Crusaders learned with surprise that the Arabs were a cultured people. They learned that the Arabs took good scientific ideas from the civilizations of various countries. They knew more about astronomy, mathematics, medicine, and geography than most Western Europeans did. In their schools, they studied old Greek and Roman writers, including Aristotle. When the Crusaders observed the benefits of education and technology in the East, they began to have a renewed interest in learning.

Some Dates to Remember

You see that Europeans were beginning to think about a number of things. Some time around A.D.1300 to 1400, a new age was born. You can think of the Renaissance, the awakening, as closing the Middle Ages and opening the modern period of history. Historians cannot fix exact dates, but the awakening and the Protestant Reformation were at their height between 1400 and 1600. Keep in mind that some of the events described in this chapter and the next began or took place during the late Middle Ages.

LANGUAGE BUILDING

Modern Language

Those who received any education during the Middle Ages learned Latin as well as their native speech. Church services were in Latin. Books and legal papers were written in Latin. Even today, many legal and medical terms are derived from the ancient Latin language.

By A.D.1400, the world was changing. Here and there, nations were taking shape. Also, writers were using their native language rather than Latin. Because of this, the Renaissance brought modern languages of two kinds into common usage—German and Roman based languages. The Germanic peoples improved their speech, as well as their entire culture, after they turned from the chaos of pagan superstitions and embraced the Christian faith. As the Germanic people began to engage in civilized behavior, they found the need to communicate clearly, and in written fashion, among their various tribes. Over time, the different variations of German and Roman-based languages, including English, began to take on their own separate identities. Even though each language eventually gained its own identity, they still share the same German and Roman roots.

The languages which are based on the Latin language are called *Romance* languages. The most common Romance languages came out of Italy, Spain, France, Portugal, and Romania (which was Romanized under Emperor Trajan during the second and third centuries A.D.) These countries were once part of the Roman Empire, where people spoke Latin. These groups of people had separate languages because they spoke Latin in different ways and became isolated from each other after the fall of the Western Roman Empire. They might use the same word but may not say it in the same way.

CANAANITE-PHOENICIAN	EARLY GREEK	LATER GREEK	LATIN	ENGLISH
ⲕ ⲁ	Δ	Δ	A	A
𝟿 𝟿	S 𝟿	Ᏸ	B	B
⌐	𝟏	⌐	C G	C, G
⌂ ⌂	Δ	Δ	D	D
⋺⋺	⋺	Ᏼ	E	E
Ⲩ	Ⲩ	Ⲩ	F V	F, U, V, W, Y
ⲍ ⲍ	I	I		Z
Ᏸ Ᏸ	𝟠	𝟠	H	H
⊗	⊗	⊗		(Th)
⏗	⏗	⏗	I	I, J
Ⲕ Ⲩⲩ	Ⲕ	k		K
ⳑⳑ	ⳟ⏋	⌐⌐	L	L
ⲙ ⲙ	ⲙ	ⲙ	M	M
Ⲩ ⲏ	Ⲩ	N	N	N
ⲭ ⲭⲭ	王	王	X	(X)
ⲟⲟ	ⲟ	ⲟ	O	O
⌐⌐⌐	⌐	⌐	P	P
ⲛⲛⲛ	Ⲙ	Ⲙ		(S)
ⳁⳁⳁ	Φ	Φ	Q	Q
ⲁ	ⲁ	ⲣ	R	R
Ⲱ	ⳍ	ⳍ	S	S
Ⲭ	T	T	T	T

Our alphabet came from the Romans. The Romans borrowed parts of their alphabet from the Greeks. What letters in the Roman alphabet are like those in the Greek alphabet? The Greeks borrowed their alphabet from the Phoenicians.

Effects of Daily Speech

Writers of the Renaissance lived in many parts of Europe. Each spoke his language somewhat differently from people in other parts of his country. When he sat down to write a poem, story, or play, he could use Latin or his native language. Many chose to use their own language, although Latin remained the common language used by scholars and scientists until the eighteenth century.

When writers desired to write in their own country's language, they began by selecting words and arranging those words in sentences in such a way that readers would understand their ideas. The next task was for the writer to spell words, which up to that point had only been spoken. This was often difficult because no one had established standards or guidelines for spelling before this early period.

It was often the case that when another writer would copy someone else's writing, he would only accept certain spellings. He would also arrange the words in sentences or phrases in his own way. Obviously, this made written communication very awkward and confusing because sentence structure was almost nonexistent and people would often spell the same word several different ways.

Effect of a Dictionary

As more and more Europeans began to make the effort to communicate with each other in writing, scholars began to put together dictionaries for the new European languages. They began by choosing the spelling that seemed best to them. They found among the country's writings those ways of expressing ideas that seemed most pleasing. They set up *standards*. After that, writers used the dictionary spellings, meanings, and samples of writing as guides in their own work.

The Revival of Classic Literature

You can see at once that the Renaissance writers did a wonderful thing for language. By writing in the language of the people, they made modern languages truly useful.

As learning and modern languages developed, more people had the desire to read the great writings of both religious and secular authors. During the Golden Ages of Rome and Greece, writers were read and talked about by educated people. Then, during the barbarian invasions, the Latin and Greek writings were lost or hid away and copied in monasteries.

In the Middle Ages, books were very rare and expensive. This is one of the reasons why poor children seldom had educational opportunities.

In the fourteenth century, a number of Italian writers discovered the ideas and beautiful writing in some old Greek and Roman manuscripts, including copies of the Old and New Testaments. They copied old manuscripts and asked their friends to read them. Soon old writings were being dug out of many hiding places.

What was it in these old books that men of the Renaissance liked? One thing was the way the Greeks wrote about their everyday lives. The Roman Catholic Church had taught people during the Middle Ages to think more of the life after death, and actually discouraged ordinary people from reading even portions of the Greek or Latin New Testament, which gives the reader a wealth of wisdom for everyday life. In spite of this discouragement, many people began to read the writings of Greek and Roman scholars.

A Famous Bible

Toward the end of the Renaissance, in 1611, the best Bible scholars in England put the Bible into English by utilizing the original Hebrew and Greek manuscripts. They did such a good job of using the finest English that this Bible became a guide for English writers. Since it was prepared with the authorization of James I, this Bible is called the King James Version. Even today it remains an enduring classic of great English literature as well as divinely inspired truth.

Perhaps the best translation of a Bible into English was done by an assembly of scholars, known as the Westminster Assembly, in 1611, during the reign of King James.

A Great English Writer

The Renaissance came late to England, but in many ways this was to the advantage of the English, for they received the writings of the best Renaissance writers tempered by the writings of great Bible scholars from the Reformation era. During the sixteenth century in England, a man named William Shakespeare was born. He has been called the master of all English writers. Some of the plays written for the theater by William Shakespeare are performed today by high school and college students. You can also see these plays on television and in the movies. There are funny plays, sad plays, and plays about people who were important in history.

A New Interest in Art

Three Famous Artists

Some of the best paintings in today's art galleries were painted during the Renaissance. Among the great Renaissance artists were three men whose work you will encounter for the rest of your life as you study art or visit art museums.

Let us pretend that you are traveling back in time to meet with a guide from the late Renaissance era who is ready to show you some scenes from the lives of three famous artists.

Statue of David the Shepherd Boy by Michelangelo

The Shepherd Boy, David

It is May 1504. You stand on a terrace before a palace in Florence, Italy. The sculptor, Michelangelo, sits frowning while other artists make speeches. "You are about to see one of the great statues of all time," they say.

Watch! Coverings are slowly pulled from a statue of the watchful shepherd, David. He is ready to fight the giant, Goliath. The boyish figure stands eighteen feet tall, three times as tall as a man. Michelangelo has carved it from one block of marble.

Pictures on a Chapel Ceiling

Now you are in Rome. The year is 1512. You enter one end of a huge chapel. A platform or scaffold fills the other end. Lying on his back on the platform is Michelangelo. He is at least sixty feet above the floor. He paints with rapid strokes on the wet plaster of the ceiling. Stretching back across the ceiling are scenes from the Bible.

From where you stand you can see scores of people told about in the Bible. They appear to be life size. As you figure out the stories told by the pictures, Michelangelo climbs down from the platform and talks with you.

"The figures appear life-size here," he agrees. "But if you could climb to my high perch, you would see that they are very large. When I look at them close at hand they seem colossal."

"Have you no helpers?" you ask.

"I have only those who prepare the wet plaster and bring me supplies," the artist replies. "I began the work more than four years ago. Soon afterward, I brought a number of painters from Florence to help me. They could not carry out my designs. They could not get enough feeling into their work or show what each person is thinking. I dismissed them and did the painting myself. I have sat or lain in that position so long that nothing looks right when I stand up."

As you leave the chapel, your guide says, "These paintings are all the more wonderful when you realize Michelangelo thinks of himself as a sculptor. He did not want to paint, but the pope insisted."

The "Last Supper"

Now you are in Milan. The year is 1498. You enter the refectory of a monastery. The day's work is done. Leonardo da Vinci is cleaning his brushes.

"You have come just in time," he says. "In a day or two, I shall put the last touches on the *Last Supper*. See how I have treated this world-shaking event. Jesus has just shocked his apostles by saying, 'One of you shall betray Me.' Have I caught the feelings of fear, wonder, and questioning that sweep over the little group?"

Your guide says, "You have, you have! It is indeed a masterpiece. I like the way you have framed the head and shoulders of the Master in the center window."

A Man of Ideas

Many years later, you go to Leonardo's workshop to learn about his scientific studies. "I could not paint well had I not discovered certain facts about light, shade, and other things in nature," he says. "Now I am trying to turn my discoveries into inventions others can use.

"For example, I believe man can fly in the air like a bird some day. I have studied the way birds fly. See my model flying boats. This one would fly if I had some kind of power for it. I know about steam, but it will not do.

"Here is a sketch of a *parachute* I have designed. I call it a 'tent roof.' With a tent roof a man can drift slowly to the ground from the air.

"Here is a sketch of my latest weapon. I have mounted a row of guns on wheels so a small crew can shoot one gun after another quickly."

As you leave the workshop, your guide says, "Leonardo is a man with ideas ahead of his time. He is a painter, poet, sculptor, architect, inventor, engineer, and musician. His notebooks are full of sketches for works of art, toys, and useful inventions."

The Third Giant

Most of you know about a painting called the *Madonna*. A 'Madonna' is a painting or statue of a mother and small child representing Mary and the baby Jesus. The Renaissance artist most famous for Madonnas was Raphael. His "Sistine Madonna" is so wonderful that it was hung alone in a large museum room.

Cathedral Building

Each medieval monastery and village had a chapel. Towns that had a bishop called their chapel a cathedral. To honor their bishop, people often tried to build a very fine cathedral. Since nearly every person belonged to the church, everyone helped with building. Craftsmen often did their finest work on their cathedrals.

Since few people could read in those days, ideas from the Bible were used as church decorations. Bible stories were painted on inside walls and shown in stained-glass windows. Carved figures represented biblical characters.

The famous Italian artist and inventor Leonardo da Vinci painted many fine works of art. The painting shown above is the Mona Lisa *and it is perhaps his most famous masterpiece.*

SCIENCE AND INVENTION

A Road to Science

Before the Renaissance, most people in the West knew very little about the natural world about them. Men called *alchemists* tried to uncover secrets of nature that today are clear to scientists. For example, alchemists experimented to find a way of changing common metals into gold. They failed, but their studies of the changes in substances prepared the way for our science of chemistry.

A Man Before His Time

During the thirteenth century, some teachers began the hard work of studying nature and teaching people facts. Among these was Roger Bacon, an English monk. Bacon taught at Oxford University. Let your imaginary guide take you to Bacon's laboratory there. The monk is experimenting with a simple steam engine when you enter.

"As my visitors probably know, the famous Aristotle wrote about the earth and the heavens," Bacon says. "His writings have been used as textbooks for hundreds of years. It may be all right to read Aristotle, but we should check his facts and ideas by experiments. We should gain new knowledge, too.

"Here in the quiet of my laboratory I can experiment, watch, record what happens, and experiment again. I have been able to give the world new facts about light and lenses. A *lens* is a piece of glass cut so that it helps us to see more clearly. I have been able to make a simple microscope and a crude telescope to help me in my work. I have worked with magnets until I have perfected a compass. Now I am experimenting with steam and my steam engine."

"Have you given these inventions to the world?" someone asks.

The friar looks at the guide with troubled eyes. The guide says, "That he cannot do now. In these days, when people are so superstitious, new ideas are thought to be sinful. People would say Friar Bacon learned from the devil. How else could he know more than other people? You see, the good friar is a man ahead of his time."

Friar Bacon nods his head and says, "If men would learn to experiment and observe, they could invent all kinds of useful things. The time will come when ships will go without rowers, and with only one man to guide them. Carriages may be made which can be moved without animals. Flying machines are possible in which a man sits and turns some device that makes wings strike the air in the manner of a bird. Machines will raise great weights."

Bacon's writings helped other men to analyze facts and create new inventions, in spite of the fact that the head of his religious order eventually imprisoned Bacon for his ideas and writings. It is sad to reflect upon how often the progress of scientific discovery has been hindered by both pagan and religious superstitions that have no basis in biblical truth.

A Discovery About the Earth

Night after night a priest named Copernicus watched the sky from a cathedral tower. Most people of the fifteenth century believed as the ancient Greeks did that the sun, moon, and stars moved around the earth. Copernicus decided this was not true. Instead, it seemed to him that the sun was the center of the universe. The earth and the other planets were spinning about the sun.

When Copernicus was sure he was right, he wrote a book so other men might study his ideas. The pope would not accept these ideas. He told Copernicus not to have the book printed. Some friends had it printed, and gave Copernicus a copy just before he died. Roman Catholic churchmen did not agree with his ideas, but many men read the book. Some thought he might be correct.

Galileo Believes Copernicus

A wise university teacher named Galileo believed the ideas of Copernicus and taught them to his classes.

Like Copernicus, Galileo looked for a way to prove the new ideas. One day he was told how a maker of eyeglasses had invented a spyglass, or telescope, in Holland. Galileo set to work to make a telescope. He ground pieces of glass, curving them in and out. Then he fitted two pieces of ground glass into a piece of organ pipe. One glass curved in and the other curved out. The new telescope made things appear three times closer. Galileo improved this tool until he had one that made objects seem thirty-two times nearer.

When Galileo studied the heavens with his spyglass, he saw many surprising things. They showed that some of men's beliefs about the heavens were wrong. Some men refused to look through the telescope. Can you imagine! They did not want to change their beliefs about the planets and stars!

Galileo experimented with many other ideas. Let your guide take you to watch one test. You join a group of teachers, priests, and students near the leaning tower of Pisa in Italy.

"Galileo believes Aristotle was wrong in saying a ten-pound weight falls ten times as fast as a one-pound weight," your guide says. "He believes that the earth has a power called *gravity*. He believes gravity pulls every object to earth with the same speed."

Galileo experimented and made a telescope before he proved the planets move around the sun.

Galileo leans out of the tower. He drops a one-pound weight and a ten-pound weight at the same time. You see them strike the earth together. You let out a cheer, but most of those who watch are quiet. They do not like to see anyone question the word of Aristotle. You find it hard to believe a grape falls as fast as a steel ball. You decide to go home and try Galileo's experiment yourself.

Bacon, Copernicus, and Galileo made many other men think. They showed that there were many things to learn which were not explained in old Greek and Latin manuscripts. They led other men to use the "scientific method"—to experiment, observe, record what happens, experiment again. This method of finding answers to questions, coupled with a faith that can assume an absolute reliability to the created order, has brought most of the inventions which make living pleasant today.

The Art of Printing

During the Renaissance men learned to print books instead of copy manuscripts by hand. The Chinese had learned to print with movable type several hundred years earlier. But there is no evidence that Europeans learned from the Chinese. The earliest examples we have of European printing are pictures printed from wooden blocks. Sometimes words were carved on the blocks and paper was laid over the block after ink was applied to its surface.

Early efforts at printing utilized carved wooden blocks or single letters. Wooden letters did not work well for several reasons.

Before printing could be made cheaper and more useful, however, a problem had to be solved. How could one make copies of pages without having to carve an entire block of wood for each page? Perhaps more than one man worked on this problem. However, historians believe Johann Gutenberg finally found the answer in Germany during the middle of the fifteenth century.

Wouldn't you have liked to be Gutenberg's assistant during the years he was figuring out how to print books from movable type? Try to picture yourself in that position as we proceed to imagine what it must have been like to work alongside Gutenberg.

Movable Letters

"I want to print a Bible," Gutenberg tells you. "That means we must carve the letters of a whole page on one block of wood. Then we must ink each block and press paper against it. It will take us forever to make one Bible that way. There must be a quicker way."

One day while he is carving blocks for a picture book, an idea comes to Gutenberg. "Why not create each letter of the alphabet on a separate block?" he asks. "Then we can arrange the letters in words and sentences. When we finish using the small wooden letters for one book, we can set them for another."

You cut boards into small pieces and carve a letter on each piece. You set letters side by side to form words. Then you put the words in a frame. When you try printing, you find the letters are not all the same height, and they, therefore, break quite easily.

Metal Type

Gutenberg says, "I have made a printer's alphabet all right, but I see wooden letters will not do. We must make our type out of metal."

Gutenberg has had experience working with metals, so he begins experimenting. He finally puts together several materials that harden into a good metal for type. He takes a good example of hand-writing and makes patterns of each letter. You cast them in molds. Now you have metal letters you can use over and over.

You realize you need some way of putting pressure more evenly on the type. Gutenberg says, "People squeeze the water from cheese with a press. They use a press to squeeze the juice from grapes. Why can't we use a press to get a clearer impression of each page of type?"

He has someone make a simple press. You set a frame of type in the press and ink the letters' faces. You lay a piece of paper over the type. You turn the screw until the paper is pressed tightly against the type. Then you lay this printed sheet aside to dry. You can make as many copies as you wish before you go on to another page.

When all the sheets of a book are printed and bound together, you have a cheaper book than anyone can make by hand. The time will come when you can print a book as large as the Bible, making more than one at a time.

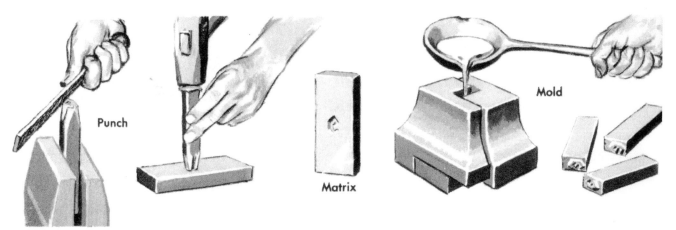

A major breakthrough in printing came about with the invention of metal type. Letters were shaped on a thin bar of steel called a punch. Each letter was then punched into soft metal to form a matrix. The matrix was slid into a mold, and hot metal was poured in. Many copies could be made or cast from one matrix to another.

Printing and Civilization

No one can estimate the importance of printing to civilization. Some historians go so far as to say printing is the world's greatest invention for freeing men's minds. Think of the newspapers, magazines, and books in your home, your school, and your library. What would your life be like without them? More importantly, where would the human race be if people could not read for themselves the inspired and infallible Word of God? Actually, we already know the answer to this last question, for before the Bible was printed in sufficient quantity during the Middle Ages, men stumbled in the darkness of sin. Of the making of books, there is no end, but the Holy Scriptures alone are truly a lamp for man's feet and a light for his path.

Help for Seamen

As you will see in the next chapter, the Renaissance was also a time of seeking new trade routes. This was in part possible because of the compass. Men had known for a long time that a piece of iron could be so treated that it would point north and south if it could swing freely. The Chinese first invented the floating compass during the early Middle Ages. It was not until around A.D. 1050, however, that Mediterranean seamen began to successfully use a magnetic compass.

At first they floated pieces of magnetized iron on cork or straw in a bowl of water. With such a guide, seamen could cross the seas without fear of becoming lost. They no longer needed to hug the coast, where they were in danger of attack by pirates.

Gunpowder

Gunpowder is a mixture of chemicals, which burns so quickly that it explodes with great force. Although gunpowder was first produced by Chinese inventors, the first military use of gunpowder on a wide scale took place in Europe. When a German monk discovered how to use the gunpowder to throw an iron ball from a cannon, gunpowder became very important. Soon Europeans were making cannons for use in war.

When guns with powder first exploded, armored knights were soon outmoded.

Then, when a noble rebelled against his king, the king's soldiers could use cannon balls and gunpowder to break down his castle walls. After the gun was invented, the common foot soldier could shoot an armored knight. Weapons and warfare were soon changed as castles and suits of armor were abandoned. Can you understand how gunpowder changed warfare and helped to end feudalism by forcing people to move away from societies that revolved around castle dwellings?

The Renaissance and You

You have seen that men of the Renaissance changed their thinking and made splendid gifts to civilization in art, education, and invention. Your lives are richer and more beautiful today because of the cathedrals they built, the paintings and sculpture they left, and the ideas they set down in their writings.

These things are important gifts from the Old World and we are grateful to God for opening men's minds to discover hidden truths. The fact that men of the Renaissance began to think carefully and to explore seriously the mysteries of God's universe was indeed a positive change. Notice how these men began to ask questions and try out new ideas. They experimented, observed, and made a record of what happened, and then experimented again.

Problems Amidst Progress

The Renaissance era was a time when European culture began to blossom on many levels. It was not, however, a trouble-free period of history. A deadly and highly contagious disease or plague began to spread throughout much of Europe between 1347 and 1352. This wide-spread and deadly plague, known as The Black Death, was the most awful natural disaster in European history and eventually killed around thirty percent of the population of Europe. It also caused the deaths of millions of Muslims living in the areas of North Africa and the Near East. Although this particular plague was not the first or last of its kind, it certainly was the worst in European history.

The great plague or Black Death is believed to have been brought to Europe aboard merchant ships that unknowingly contained disease-carrying rats. The merchant ships landed at a port in Sicily and the rats managed to get to shore when the cargo was unloaded. Within a few weeks, people began to get sick and die as they were exposed to the deadly bacteria that the rats helped to spread. At one point during the height of the plague, some major European cities reported almost 1,000 deaths per day.

As you might well imagine, The Black Death had enormous effects upon the later Renaissance period. Many

The plague known as the Black Death (1347-51) began when disease-carrying rats came ashore in port cities along the Mediterranean Sea in southern Europe. This horrible plague wiped out one third of the population of Europe.

people believed that the plague was a form of Divine punishment or chastening and so those who survived The Black Death were inclined to be more religious than they were before. In addition, the mere fact that so many people of working age died had a serious effect on the economy of various European nations. Many skilled workers and craftsmen were no longer around to produce goods and services. In areas where the plague hit the hardest, even food production was affected for a time as farm workers were often in short supply.

In spite of this difficult trial, the people of Europe were able to eventually get their lives and economics back in good order. By God's grace, some good developments came out of the hard times of sickness. For one thing, the hearts of people were more open to spiritual truths and eternal considerations, which helped to set the stage for the great Protestant Reformation. Also, the devastating effects of plague began to cause men to investigate the issues of public health and medical science with greater diligence. Before the great plague, few people were concerned about public health standards or the study of the prevention or treatment of disease among human beings. The Black Death also hastened the end of the old feudal system. As workers became scarce and, therefore, more valuable they could find work almost anywhere they wished to travel. Feudal lords could no longer hold their serfs under their firm control for they were now able to gain wealth apart from their masters.

CHAPTER SUMMARY

The Crusades had shown Western Europeans that the Byzantines and Arabs had more culture and learning than they had. Men who attended the Moors' universities also came home with new ideas. Soon men were asking questions about many things and reaching out for better ways of living.

A great change came over western Europe. Thousands of men flocked to the universities. The writings and art of ancient Greeks and Romans were rediscovered and studied. Painters and sculptors gave the world many pictures and statues to enjoy. Many writers began to turn away from Latin and to write good books in the language of their people. Scientists discovered new things about our world by using a scientific method. This standard method is as important to us as any Renaissance invention because it helps us to gather information that can be used to solve mysteries or problems in the physical world.

This great awakening to new ways of living and thinking is called the Renaissance. The Renaissance began in the late Middle Ages and carried over into the Reformation era we are about to study. During this period, feudalism died. There were changes in government and religion. Inventions helped men sail the seas and discover new lands. People learned to think, experiment, observe, and experiment again. Out of this great awakening came many ideas and things that enrich our lives today such as printing presses, telescopes, and the Holy Bible printed in the common languages of the people of many nations.

This map shows the most important countries and cities of Europe, and the neighboring lands of Africa and Asia, as they were about the year A.D. 1200.

Leonardo da Vinci was not only a great painter, but a gifted inventor. Here he is seen in his workshop testing his idea of a parachute. Sketches of other inventions lay scattered about. Notice the models of a flying machine, a helicopter, and a machine gun.

CHAPTER QUESTIONS AND ACTIVITIES

1. What things happened that awoke a new interest in learning among Europeans?

2. Between what dates was this awakening at its height?

3. Why are some languages called Germanic languages and some called Romance languages?

4. How did Renaissance writers help build modern languages? How did the dictionary makers help?

5. What was it in Greek manuscripts that men of the Renaissance liked?

6. Why is the King James Version of the Bible still popular?

7. What artist painted Bible pictures on a chapel ceiling in Rome?

8. Who liked to paint Madonnas?

9. Who painted the "Last Supper"?

10. Why do people who visit Europe like to see the great cathedrals?

11. Why was Roger Bacon called "a man ahead of his time"?

12. Besides Roger Bacon, what great Renaissance thinker believed that man would someday fly?

13. Name four steps taken by men who use a scientific method to explore the physical world.

14. Why was the printing press one of the greatest inventions of all time?

15. How did the compass help sailors?

16. You will want to see a modern printing press in action. You can plan a class visit to your local newspaper pressroom or to a printing plant.

17. If there is an art museum near your home, you can probably arrange for a visit and lecture on Renaissance art.

18. If you get copies of pictures by Renaissance painters, you can stage an art exhibit. You can add models of famous Renaissance sculptures you carve from white soap.

19. Perhaps you can talk with someone who has visited Europe to tell you about the cathedrals and other sights he enjoyed in Europe.

KEY TERMS

Alchemist	Madonna
Gravity	Renaissance
Lens	Standards

WHAT THE MIDDLE AGES DID FOR LATER TIMES

The fine customs of chivalry which developed during the Middle Ages form the basis for the polite behavior of gentlemen today.

Many of the lines of business started in the Middle Ages have developed into great industries of today.

During the Middle Ages the monks wrote down in books much knowledge from past ages and saved it for later times.

The builders in the Middle Ages developed Gothic architecture, which is still used for many of our most beautiful buildings.

Chapter 11
THE PROTESTANT REFORMATION

Unworthy Churchmen

As the monasteries and churches of the Middle Ages grew, they gained control of great stretches of land. In time, the Church of Rome became very rich. Power-loving rulers and nobles wanted to control the church lands. To accomplish this purpose, they often persuaded greedy relatives and friends to become ministers of the Roman Catholic Church and then helped them to become bishops. And so, these unworthy leaders used their offices to enrich themselves at the expense of God's truth and God's people.

It had long been customary for the Church to encourage people to show that they were really sorry for their sins by doing good deeds or by contributing money for some worthy cause. This custom was often used by unscrupulous churchmen to increase their wealth. In exchange for donations from church members, for example, these unfaithful churchmen often sold wrongdoers pieces of parchment called indulgences, that promised the purchasers forgiveness of sin even if they had not repented of their misdeeds.

Good and sincere churchmen were displeased with the idleness and wickedness of these unfaithful bishops. The church leaders at Rome, however, were unwilling to discipline or dismiss the dishonorable bishops and priests.

Kings and the Pope

During the latter part of the Middle Ages, the people in the various countries of Europe began to form nations. For example, the people of England came to look upon themselves as a united people. They wanted to be independent of other peoples. They wanted to be governed only by their own rulers and not by anyone who lived outside the boundaries of England.

The pope, on the other hand, at that time considered himself ruler over all kings. There was often trouble between the pope and the kings of the various nations. As the feeling of national unity and national pride grew stronger in each of the European nations, the people often sided with their king against the pope. In Germany the people were not united into a strong nation, but there, too, in the quarrels between the pope and the emperor, people often sided against the pope. So it was that during the latter part of the Middle Ages many rulers and many people were becoming unwilling that the pope should take part in the government of their countries.

The New Learning

For many years, churchmen were almost the only people who could read. They alone had Bibles to read, for there were very few books. For years they had passed on to the people the teachings of the Bible that apply to all areas of life such as family life, church life, and civil matters.

But during the latter part of the Middle Ages, there was a new interest in learning. More and more people learned how to read. Schools and universities were established in Europe that often had only a loose connection to the Roman Catholic Church.

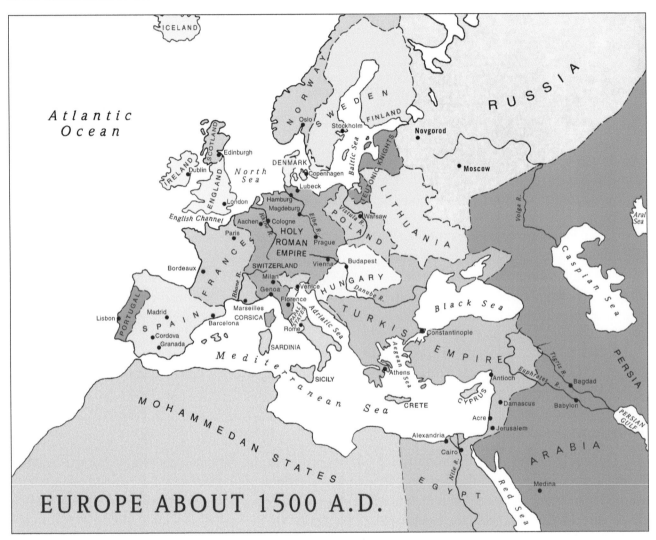

EUROPE ABOUT 1500 A.D.

The teachers and students at these universities spent much time in studying and discussing religious matters. Some of them disagreed with specific teachings of the Roman church leaders and believed they were unbiblical. Some men at the universities became very outspoken against certain teachings and practices of churchmen and made further calls for reform.

An English Bible

John Wycliffe, born in 1330, was a teacher at Oxford University. He is known in history as the Morning Star of the Reformation because he was one of the first to speak out against the selfish men in church offices. He saw that many churchmen were rich and powerful feudal lords, little interested in the spiritual or physical welfare of the people. He said that in the eyes of God all men are equal; that priests should live simply and humbly like the Lord Jesus did; and that all church leaders, including the pope, should be subject to the Word of God.

Like all Christians, Wycliffe loved the Bible. He believed that everyone should read the Bible for himself and learn its teachings from his own reading. But at this time the Bible was written only in Latin. Most of the people could not read Latin, and many of them could not read at all. Furthermore, the Church of Rome had a longstanding law that forbade anyone from printing the Bible in English or in any other language beside Latin. The pope did not want ordinary people to study the Bible for fear that he would lose control over the people and permit them to challenge Rome's view of the Scripture. In spite of Rome's opposition, Wycliffe and his followers translated the Bible into English so that those who could read might read it for themselves. Then he sent his followers, known as Lollards, out to villages and towns to read the Bible in English to those who could not read, and to help the poor and needy. In just a few years, the people of England began to grow in the grace and knowledge of God, free to think God's thoughts after Him.

Thanks to the efforts of John Wycliffe, the people of England were able to hear the Bible read aloud in their own language for the first time. The followers of Wycliffe were known as the Lollards. They traveled throughout England reading the Scriptures to the common people.

A Monk Speaks Out

Wycliffe's ideas and writings reached John Huss, a monk and teacher in Bohemia. Like Wycliffe, Huss believed that everyone should read the Bible and think for himself about Jesus' teachings. He translated the Bible into Czech, the language of his people.

Huss was a powerful preacher, much loved by his followers. When he spoke out against some of the practices in the Roman Catholic Church, he was tried before a church council. He was found guilty of criticizing accepted church beliefs and was burned at the stake.

We must not think that all the people who opposed the pope and the church were good people, willing to let everyone believe as he wished, and that all those who remained loyal to the pope and the church were bad people, cruel to anyone who disagreed with them. Such was, indeed, not the case. There were good and bad people on both sides, and on both sides there were people who believed it was their duty to kill anyone who disagreed with their religious beliefs. Nevertheless, men like Wycliffe and Huss did the right thing in courageously and boldly risking their lives to give people the opportunity to read the Bible for themselves. All lovers of truth and liberty should thank God for the work of these early Church reformers.

A Popular Teacher

Martin Luther was born in Germany about a hundred years after Wycliffe died. He was nine years old when Columbus set foot on the Americas in 1492.

Martin was a bright child, eager to learn and full of questions. His parents worked hard to send him to the university. They hoped he would be a lawyer. After Martin had a narrow escape from death as a young man, he became determined to enter a monastery. There he spent hours in prayer, fasting, and useful labor. He lived according to the rules of the monastery and was a faithful monk, although no amount of good works or prayers could give him peace of mind or soul.

After three years in the monastery, Luther was sent to teach in the university at Wittenberg. There he became very popular with his students. Since he was teaching religion, he did much thinking about certain practices within the Church and also probed into the question of how a wicked sinner like himself could become just in the sight of a holy God.

Some Famous Objections

At about this time, the pope began to plan to complete the Church of St. Peter at Rome. A lot of money was needed for this building project.

A monk named Tetzel was in charge of raising money in Wittenberg. He was so eager to get the money that he seemed to care little about how he accomplished his purpose. To him, the most important duty was to obtain money for the great temple in Rome. To accomplish this, he distorted the Church's teaching. He sold pieces of parchment, called *indulgences,* on which promises were written guaranteeing forgiveness without requiring repentance.

It was the custom of that day to write out statements of things one wanted to debate with other scholars. Luther sat down and wrote out what he believed about Tetzel's efforts to raise

A monk named Martin Luther challenged some of the teachings and practices of the Roman Catholic Church. He nailed his objections, called the ninety-five theses, on a church door at Wittenburg, Germany. These written objections were widely copied and distributed throughout Europe.

money, as well as several other problems he recognized in Roman Catholic doctrine. Then he nailed a copy of his theological challenge, known as the *Ninety-five Theses*, to the door of the church at Wittenberg. He hoped in this way to start discussion among the students and teachers as to whether or not the teachings or practices of the Church in specific areas were biblically correct.

Printing Steps In

Luther started a discussion all right, not only among Wittenberg teachers and students, but also in all of northern Europe. He was a loyal churchman. He had no idea that his objections would tear apart the Roman Catholic Church. But he did not fully understand the power of the printing press. His statements were put in pamphlet form and sent all over Germany. In less than two-months' time, they were being talked about in England, France, and Italy. The university press was kept busy making copies of the now famous objections, or arguments, as well as with printing other writings from Dr. Martin Luther.

Many teachers and students at Wittenberg agreed with Luther, but they did not debate his statements in public. While discussion of Tetzel's use of indulgences was going on, Luther began talking and writing about other church practices which he believed should be corrected or reformed.

His study of church law, church history, and the Bible made Luther feel that the Church was wrong in some of its doctrines. In one public debate he went so far as to say that the pope should not have so much power. He wrote more of his ideas. Again the power of the printed word was shown. Luther's ideas were printed in three powerful pamphlets.

Luther Must Decide

The pope wrote a letter in which he told Luther that he must take back, or *recant,* what he had written. Luther must also burn the books and pamphlets he had written. If Luther did not recant, the pope would remove or excommunicate him from the Church.

One December evening in 1520, a crowd gathered around a bonfire in Wittenberg. There were teachers, students, and others in the crowd. "Will Luther obey the pope?" was the question in everyone's mind.

Luther appeared carrying some books and papers. People nudged each other. "He is going to burn his writings," they whispered.

The unhappy priest walked to the fire. As the light from the fire shone upon the books, they saw that these were not Luther's writings. Good heavens! He carried the pope's letter and the law of the Roman Catholic Church! While the silent crowd looked on in awe, Luther threw these into the fire. Luther then said, "The pope's letter condemns me without any proof from Scripture. If I am a heretic, then let him show me from God's Word. It is better that I die a thousand times than I should retract one word of what I have written about the sacred truth of God."

Luther Is Tried

The pope and other church leaders were greatly offended. Luther was ordered to appear before a council for trial.

Some of his friends urged him not to go. They told him about the fate of John Huss. They could not stop him. Luther went to trial even though he knew that he would likely be executed.

The council before which Luther appeared for trial was made up of members of the clergy, German princes and nobility, and the emperor. When Luther came before them, the council demanded that he recant and acknowledge that he had been wrong. Luther refused to recant. Instead, he tried to explain why he believed as he did. The council listened carefully to what Luther had to say, but its members would not agree with him. He was found guilty of preaching ideas that disagreed with the accepted teachings of the Church. He was condemned as a *heretic*—a person who taught beliefs different from those accepted as true by the Church.

A Castle Gets a Prisoner

Some people thought Luther got what he deserved, but many others did not agree. They felt that all ministers of the Gospel should have the right to appeal to the authority of the Scripture and that the Word of God was a higher authority in the Church than the pope or bishops.

The emperor had promised a noble, named Frederick III, that Luther could go home before he was executed, so Luther started for home. On the way, a band of horsemen wearing masks seized Luther. They took him to the castle of a friendly noble who wanted to save Luther's life.

While Luther was hidden at the castle, he worked hard. He translated the New Testament into the beautiful German language so that his people would be able to read it.

A New Church Is Born

You can picture the upheaval that took place in Germany. Many people believed that Luther was right. They accepted his teachings and wanted to set up a reformed church. The time came when Luther went back to Wittenberg and helped organize such a church. He helped set up a new order of church services and a form of church government that rejected the claim of the pope to be infallible and supreme. Perhaps the most fundamental reform in the Lutheran church involved the proclamation that all sinners are saved only through the grace of God by faith in the work of Christ at Calvary and not by virtue of church approval or good works.

One of the biggest changes in the worship services was to have those who attended the services sing hymns. Luther himself wrote about 125 hymns. In later years, his ideas and teachings, as well as those of other Reformers, were spread to many countries of the world.

The Reformation was a battle for the authority of Scripture over the opinions of men. In other words, it was a struggle to establish what was true and set people free. As the Bible says, "And you shall know the truth, and the truth shall make you free." John 8:32.

Other Reformers

Churchmen in many places took up the criticism of the practices of the Roman Catholic Church. Likewise, churchmen in many places defended the Church of Rome. Gradually the desire for reformed church practices spread over much of northern Europe. A number of religious groups developed, each calling itself Christian.

Because it was concerned with reforming the Church, the broad movement is called the *Reformation.* The new churches that came out of it are called *Protestant* churches. Each was a protest against certain unbiblical practices that were being carried on with the approval of the leaders of the Roman Catholic Church. In a larger sense, however, they were protests against doctrines that clearly perverted the teachings of Jesus as set down in the Bible. They were also protests against the power of the pope over the consciences of men.

Calvin and Calvinism

In the early days of the Reformation, a man named Zwingli preached in Switzerland against certain teachings of the Church. Some people agreed with him, but others did not. The two groups finally fought a civil war, during which Zwingli was killed.

At the same time, a young reformer was winning many followers in France. His name was John Calvin. The French king was a loyal Catholic, so Calvin was forced to flee to Switzerland after the French government authorized the persecution of thousands of peaceful Huguenots (French Protestants) throughout France. John Calvin settled in Geneva, which had just gained its independence from a feudal lord. By this time, the Swiss states had won the right to choose their religion.

Calvin had studied to be a priest. He knew church history and he knew law. The people of Geneva liked his ideas. In a short time, they accepted Calvin as their leader. He started a reformed church that sought to bring church and civil laws into conformity to the Bible. The city government passed laws that were more consistent to the Word of God. Regrettably, the people of Geneva were not ready for such restrictions and prohibitions. The followers of Calvin were forced to back down for a period of time, but eventually, the people of Geneva invited Calvin back and accepted much of his direction and leadership.

The writings of the great Reformation leader, John Calvin, had a major impact upon many in Europe. The English Puritans brought many of the teachings of Calvin to North America in the 1600's.

Like most of the Reformers, John Calvin was a gifted writer. This helped Reformation ideas to spread far and wide as Calvin frequently corresponded with various European monarchs over a period of many years. In 1536, he also wrote a now famous summary of key Christian doctrines, entitled *The*

Institutes of the Christian Religion, which is still regarded by many Christians as an important work on the teachings of Scripture.

Students came from all over Europe to study under Calvin. They spread his teachings to The Netherlands, Scotland, and England. His followers in England became known as Puritans; and those Puritans, who settled near Massachusetts Bay more than 400 years ago, brought many of the teachings of Calvin to America. Much of the liberty we now enjoy can be traced to the spring of Puritan theology. For example, Puritans believed that the law should be supreme and not the opinions of popes or princes. In modern times, this is referred to as the "rule of law."

The Church of England

The English king, Henry VIII, asked the pope to annul his marriage on the grounds that his wife was unable to bear him a son. The pope refused so King Henry became angry and withdrew from the Church of Rome. Henry VIII eventually helped to establish a new church for England that was independent of Rome, called the Anglican Church or the Church of England, in 1534. As the new head of the Church of England, Henry VIII suppressed the monasteries but did little else, since he wanted the English church to remain Catholic, but separate from Rome.

After Henry died, Protestant reforms were introduced while King Edward VI reigned. But in 1553, when his Catholic half-sister, Mary I, came to the throne, she persecuted the Protestants and repressed the truth. It was not until Elizabeth I became queen, in 1558, that the independent Church of England was re-established. In 1571, the teaching of the Reformation became the standard for doctrine, as formulated in The Thirty-nine Articles.

Conclusion

Under the pope, the ruler of a country was expected to see that his people were obedient Catholics. The clergy and the king told the people what to do. Often, if a ruler became a Protestant, he expected his subjects to adopt his faith, too. In the providence of God, the teachings of faithful Reformers like Luther and Calvin eventually helped to break the people free from the arbitrary rule of tyrants within the state or church. The battle cry of the Reformation was, "No other King but Jesus."

SOME RESULTS OF THE REFORMATION

Results in Europe

Many historians believe that this religious upheaval was one of the most important events in European history. As the Protestant Reformation went on, many reformed churches were organized in northern Europe. Everyone was upset, those who remained in the Roman Catholic Church and those who broke away. This unrest took the form of fear and hatred of the religious practices of neighbors. There was much bitterness and bloodshed, but in the end the Church in Rome no longer held the people in fear, ignorance, and spiritual bondage.

The Reformation greatly weakened the authority of power-hungry church leaders and re-established the supremacy of both Christ and Holy Scripture.

CHAPTER SUMMARY

The Roman Catholic Church grew to be more powerful than any government in western Europe. As the learning of the Renaissance grew, some clergy found fault with certain church practices. John Wycliffe, John Huss, and Martin Luther tried to get these practices corrected. Each put the Bible into the language of his people. The church tried and punished many of the Reformers, and Huss was burned to death.

Luther escaped and started a new church. Soon much of Europe was ready to challenge the rule of Rome. New churches were started. Catholics and Protestants fought each other. Many people ultimately fled to America, where they could worship God as they believed He required.

Martin Luther wrote over 125 hymns. The one printed here is, perhaps, his most beloved work.

A Mighty Fortress Is Our God

God is our refuge and strength, an ever-present help in trouble. Ps. 46:1

1. A might-y for-tress is our God, a bul-wark nev-er
2. Did we in our own strength con-fide, our striv-ing would be
3. And though this world, with dev-ils filled, should threat-en to un-
4. That Word a-bove all earth-ly pow'rs, no thanks to them, a-

fail-ing; our help-er he a-mid the flood of
los-ing; were not the right man on our side, the
do us, we will not fear, for God hath willed his
bid-eth; the Spir-it and the gifts are ours through

mor-tal ills pre-vail-ing. For still our an-cient foe
man of God's own choos-ing. Dost ask who that may be?
truth to tri-umph through us. The prince of dark-ness grim,
him who with us sid-eth. Let goods and kin-dred go,

doth seek to work us woe; his craft and pow'r are great;
Christ Je-sus, it is he, Lord Sa-ba-oth his name,
we trem-ble not for him; his rage we can en-dure,
this mor-tal life al-so; the bod-y they may kill:

and armed with cru-el hate, on earth is not his e-qual.
from age to age the same, and he must win the bat-tle.
for lo! his doom is sure; one lit-tle word shall fell him.
God's truth a-bid-eth still; his king-dom is for-ev-er.

Based on Psalm 46
Martin Luther, 1529
Tr. by Frederick H. Hedge, 1853

EIN' FESTE BURG 8.7.8.7.6.6.6.6.7.
Martin Luther, 1529

CHAPTER QUESTIONS AND ACTIVITIES

1. Why did some of the clergy want a Bible written in the language of the people?

2. For what was John Wycliffe known?

3. Why was John Huss put to death?

4. Why did Martin Luther criticize the Church of Rome?

5. What invention helped spread Luther's ideas through all Europe?

6. How did Luther escape being executed?

7. What did Luther do while hiding?

8. What do we call the movement to reform church practices?

9. Why were people who wanted to reform the church called Protestants?

10. What was John Calvin's major accomplishment?

11. What were the results of the Reformation?

12. Imagine yourself a student in a university during the Reformation. Tell how you feel about having the Bible and other books written in your native language instead of Latin.

13. To get a picture of the places where the Reformation began, you can use an outline map of Europe. Locate the places where Wycliffe, Huss, Luther, Zwingli, and Calvin taught. The encyclopedias will help you with place names.

14. The religious leaders of long ago led very active and interesting lives. You might look up the life of one leader and report to your parents.

KEY TERMS

Heretic	Reformation
Protestant	Excommunicate
Recant	Indulgences

Chapter 12

EXPLORATION AND DISCOVERY

The Reformation Spurs Exploration

As you have already learned, the great teachings of the Reformation helped to refocus and enrich the period of awakening that historians call the Renaissance. The great Protestant Reformers taught the people that all honest work, if done to the glory of God, was dignified and meaningful. They also challenged Christians to take the Great Commission of Jesus Christ seriously, and to begin to go into all the world with the Gospel, or Good News, that Jesus is the Way of salvation, the Truth from God, and the Life everlasting.

The zeal that many adventurous people had in Europe to bring glory to God and wealth to their respective homelands was a prime reason why a number of them began to explore unknown parts of the world. In addition to these factors, the end of the Middle Ages was also a time when many nations in Europe were looking for a better way to trade goods with countries in Asia like India or China. The old overland trade routes were very slow and often dangerous due to the fact that most of the routes went through lands that were now under Muslim control.

Trading Becomes Easier by Water

Just at the time when adventurous sea captains and zealous missionaries were interested in traveling to far away places, a great number of improvements had recently been made which caused sailing to be less difficult and dangerous. Ships were designed to be bigger, stronger, and faster. Improvements in map and sail making, better navigation tools, such as compasses and spyglasses, and better knowledge of astronomy helped make long voyages to distant lands safer and quicker.

Above are shown older forms of the compass, rudder, and sails. Below are the boxed compass, new rudder, and improved sails that made possible the voyages of men like Columbus and da Gama.

An Inside Look at the Growing Trade Business

As we continue through this chapter, we will pretend that we are reading the newspaper column of a traveling news reporter who lived during the latter part of the Middle Ages. Please stay alert, however, for this roving reporter travels very fast from place to place. If you do pay attention, this reporter will give you a good idea of what the early period of exploration was like.

Extra! Extra! Portuguese Officials Seek New Trade Routes

As Portugal seeks to build up its foreign trade with the East, it must overcome some big obstacles. During my recent discussion with an advisor to the king of Portugal, he was quick to recognize how successful the Italian city-states of Venice and Genoa have been in building strong economies. The king himself, I was told, is convinced that these successes are directly tied to the fact that they control the sea trade with the East. In fact, he went so far as to say that since the last crusade, these Italian states have been ready to protect their trading vessels with actual warships! It was obvious to this reporter that the king and his advisor believe that the trade routes in the Mediterranean and Black Seas are deliberately kept as the private possession of the states of Italy.

The king is reported to have said, "We are doing well on the goods we bring from Africa. There must be a lot of money in bringing eastern goods into Western Europe. We must get our share of the trade with China, India, Japan, and islands of the Indies. To do so without fighting a war, we will have to find a new trade route to the East."

Prince Henry's Laboratory

After my interview with the king's advisor, I came down here to the tip of Portugal to see the king's son. Prince Henry has become interested in ships and sailing. He has built a tower on a cliff near the Atlantic Ocean so that he can easily stay in touch with the sea captains he is trying to help.

Prince Henry proves to be friendly and talkative. "My friends and I spend much of our time in this tower," he says. "As you can see, we have made many maps and charts. As our sea captains report their voyages, we are mapping the west coast of Africa and the nearby islands. We invite Portuguese mapmakers, sea captains, and sailors to study our findings. All of them help us improve our aids to navigation."

"Do you believe that the world is round?" I asked.

Prince Henry smiled. "You have been reading the Scriptures I see," he said. "We have studied the Book of Isaiah chapter 40, and old Greek and Roman manuscripts, too. Strange, isn't it, how some men lost this idea of a round world during the Dark Ages? Now one has a hard time convincing sailors that the world isn't flat and the sea full of monsters. But we are making progress. Because of our help and our sailors' study, Portugal has the best sailors in Europe. One of these days they will sail around the world and show the common sailor that the Holy Scriptures were correct all along."

A Route Around Africa

"The story has gotten around that you believe a new route to the East can be found by sailing around

Africa," I said. "Is it true that every captain tries to go farther south from Portugal on each trip down the west coast of Africa?"

"The story is true," Prince Henry says. "It may not come in my day, but as our sailors gain more courage and knowledge, one of them will sail around Africa. Then he or someone else will map a route across the ocean to India."

Spain Wants a Route, Too

During these years when Portugal's sailors have been finding a route to India, Spain has also talked about finding a route to the East. But the Spanish have been busy driving the Moors out of their country. The king has had no money for exploring around the world.

The war has been won. Now Queen Isabella and King Ferdinand can turn their attention to building up Spain. Christopher Columbus has been around again looking for help in his quest to sail to East Asia. He insists that the world is round. He has it figured out that, by sailing straight west across the Atlantic, he will reach India. He says it is about 2,400 miles from the Canary Islands to India. Some geographers laugh at him. They say it is nearer 11,000 miles.

Off for the East

Your reporter has been given the privilege of sailing with Columbus on an eventful voyage. The Spanish government has provided three small ships and made an agreement with Columbus. He is to have the title of Admiral and a share of all the goods he brings from the East.

The ships are small—the *Santa Maria*, the *Niña*, and the *Pinta*. Columbus has had a hard time rounding up enough sailors to make three crews. So many are afraid they might never come back. Columbus argues that his maps and charts and the new compass will carry us safely through. Unlike the king of Spain, I believe him.

It is now August 3, 1492. We are off for our big adventure!

Is This India?

From the beginning, this voyage has had its problems and hardships. The *Pinta* broke its steering gear and had to be repaired at the Canary Islands. Some days the wind died and the ships just drifted. Sometimes we ran into terrific storms that tossed the little ships wildly. This old Atlantic can be mighty rough.

The Middle Ages ended just as the age of exploration began. During the age of exploration, many countries in Europe sent ships to the Americas in an effort to claim territory for their respective countries.

The sailors have behaved badly because of their fear. When they refused to go farther, Columbus promised he would turn back if we did not reach Asia in a few days. They feel better today because we have seen signs of land. Columbus and a few others think they saw a tiny glimmer of light tonight. No one wants to go to bed.

Land! Land, ho! We have sighted land at two o'clock in the morning. The moon is bright and the lookout on the *Pinta* says he can make out cliffs and a dark line of land.

It is October 12, 1492. We have landed. How good it is to feel one's feet on solid ground again! With prayers of thanksgiving to God, Columbus has named this island San Salvador (Holy Savior). Columbus thinks this must be an island off the coast of India. Because of this, he calls the native people *Indians*.

Failure or Accomplishment?

I will pass over the next few years quickly. Columbus returned to Spain with the news that he had discovered a new route to India by sailing due west. All Spain went wild. The king and queen received Columbus at court and hailed him as the world's greatest seaman. They gave him better ships for another trip.

In all, he made four trips to the land he had discovered. But he found none of the splendid cities of the East. He found no spices or jewels and but little gold. The people lost interest in him. He died in 1506, broken in spirit. No one knows just what he discovered or found. Could it have been a new group of islands? Was he close to the mainland of China or India?

A New Route Is Found

Time passes. It is September, 1499. Prince Henry has been dead nearly forty years, but his forecast has come true. Today Lisbon is giving a big reception to Vasco da Gama. He has just returned from mapping a new route to India.

Others See the Americas

You will have to leave this fifteenth-century reporter and look ahead into history. You already know what he did not, that Columbus came upon two new continents lying between Europe and the East.

You also know that Columbus was not the first seaman from Europe to see the Americas. The bold Vikings under Leif Ericson had visited the shores of North America some 500 years before. But it was the trips made by Columbus that led other men to visit the New World.

The voyages of Columbus, da Gama, and others helped to make men less afraid of the sea. Being less afraid, the hope of gaining wealth or of spreading the dominion of the Christian faith drove many men to set out for the new lands.

EXPLORERS FROM SPAIN

The First Colonies

Columbus set up Spain's first colony in the Americas on the island of Hispaniola, which we now call Haiti and the Dominican Republic. After the colony was moved to a better location on the island, it became the first permanent settlement in the New World.

Spaniards were quick to explore and make more settlements in the Americas. Some came to

Hispaniola and to other islands in the West Indies. Others went into Central America, South America, and North America, in what is now the United States. The first permanent settlement in North America was at St. Augustine in the land of Florida.

An Important Discovery

Ahead of the colonists and missionaries went the Spanish explorers. All watched for a new water route to the East.

Among the explorers was a young nobleman named Vasco de Balboa. While Balboa was in charge of a Spanish colony in what is now

Long before Columbus sailed to America, Viking explorers came to North America and established temporary settlements in several areas. The first permanent settlement in North America was made by the Spanish in 1565, at St. Augustine, Florida.

Panama, an Indian told him of an ocean west of the mountains. The Indian said there was also much gold to be found in Peru, whose shores touched that ocean.

In 1513, Balboa started out with a large party of colonists and Indians. He saw the ocean from a mountaintop and four days later stood on its shores. Balboa called it the South Sea. He claimed the ocean for Spain and all the lands bordering it. Balboa's discovery proved that this was a new land and not a part of Asia.

First Trip Around the World

The Spaniards had their adventures exploring the vast New World. So did the men who looked for a waterway through the Americas to the Pacific.

In 1519, a fleet of five ships sailed from Spain on a famous voyage that lasted three years. The leader of this party was Ferdinand Magellan. He hoped to find a new route to the wealth of the East. When he reached South America, Magellan entered every river

An energetic explorer from Spain named Balboa claimed the Pacific Ocean during his trip to Central America.

mouth, looking for a waterway through the continent. One ship was lost in a storm. Another one's captain and crew turned back home.

The remaining ships sailed into a long waterway at the southern end of South America. The water was salty. Could this be a waterway through the Americas? Finally, the ships sailed out upon a broad ocean, which Magellan called the "Peaceful Sea" or Pacific. Hoping to reach some spice islands, he pushed on across the unknown sea. Food gone and men dying of hunger, Magellan came at last to a group of islands. The natives were not friendly, however, so Magellan had to sail on further.

On he pushed to the Philippines. Here food was obtained, but natives killed Magellan.

His men burned one boat and escaped to some spice islands. There they gave up another leaking ship and loaded the remaining ship with spices. Down around Africa and home to Spain went the *Victoria*. "Believe it or not," the captain said, "we have sailed around the world!"

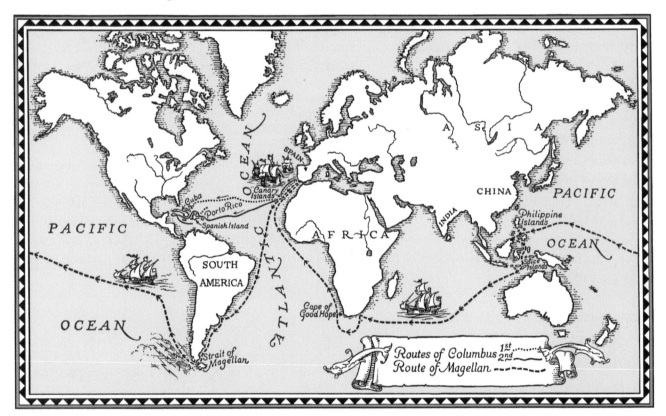

Routes of Columbus and Magellan.

Now Do You Believe?

You can imagine the excitement in the Spanish port when the *Victoria* docked. Three years ago it had sailed off into the West. Now it had come out of the East.

Ferdinand Magellan was a famous navigator and sea captain. In September, 1519, Magellan set sail from Spain with five ships on a journey to prove that ships could sail around the world. Although Magellan was killed during this voyage, his men finally made it around the entire world and back to Spain in 1522.

So Columbus and many scientists and theologians were right when they said you could reach the East by sailing West! Now even ignorant sailors or shopkeepers will have to acknowledge that the world must be round. And the land that Columbus had found was a new continent. Now men must change their ideas of world geography!

The Natives Are Robbed

Indians in the West Indies spoke of cities of gold. Where were they in Mexico? The rulers of Spain wanted gold to build more ships and expand their growing empire in the New World. One day an order came to Hernando Cortez to conquer the Aztecs in Mexico.

Cortez left Cuba in 1519, with a fleet of ships and some 500 soldiers. After he landed in Tenochtitlan, which is now called Mexico City, he was joined by Indians who hated the Aztecs. The Aztec king, Montezuma, sent presents to Cortez and then came out to meet him. The two men greeted each other politely, although each feared the other. Cortez was sickened by the sight of the pagan temples, as they regularly sacrificed human beings on their altar stones. Each month, the pagan priests, who worked for Montezuma, slaughtered thousands of innocent human beings. For this reason, when Cortez first arrived he was looked upon by many of the inhabitants as a liberator.

Cortez soon made Montezuma a prisoner in his own palace. Later on, he began collecting wealth from the Aztec cities and closing down the wicked pagan temples. The Aztecs finally revolted when Cortez's men began to mistreat them, and a bitter war followed. The capital Tenochtitlan, Mexico City, was destroyed. Cortez overcame the Aztecs and claimed Mexico for Spain. The Aztecs were put to work in the silver mines, digging more treasure for the greedy Spaniards. Priests who founded missions were about the only ones who treated the Indians decently, although it must be remembered that the Aztec tribes often treated each other very badly as well.

Peru Is Robbed

Do you remember the Indians telling Balboa there was gold in Peru? Francisco Pizarro was with Balboa in Panama and heard the story. Some time later, the Spanish king granted Pizarro the opportunity to explore and conquer Peru for Spain.

Peru turned out to be richer than Mexico. Again the natives were robbed and forced to work for the Spaniards. Much gold and silver was mined and shipped to Spain. Together, Mexico and Peru helped make Spain the richest nation in the world.

Early Spanish explorers in the New World of America often brought back spices and exotic foods as well as gold and silver.

Gold in North America

Explorers working out of the West Indies hoped to find gold in North America. Ponce de Leon found Florida and claimed it for Spain. De Soto traveled overland from Florida until he came to the Mississippi River. His men built boats and crossed the river. When they arrived in what is now Arkansas, they decided to turn back.

About this time, another Spaniard named Coronado started northward from Mexico looking for cities of gold. The Indian leaders made up stories about cities of gold in an effort to get some of the Spanish to leave Mexico. Not surprisingly, the greedy Spaniards were foolish enough to believe the stories. Coronado went at least as far as present-day Kansas but found only Indian villages. Instead of gold, Coronado gave Spain a claim to the southwestern part of North America. Even today, much of South America, Central America, and the Southwestern portion of North America are inhabited by Spanish speaking people.

EXPLORERS FROM OTHER NATIONS

French Explorers

Spain had a head start on exploring and claiming the New World because she hired explorers like Columbus. By robbing the Indians, the Spaniards also obtained money to send out many explorers. But don't think for a minute that other European nations and adventurers intended to let Spain claim all of these lands. France and England soon become very active in sending out explorers that they hoped would gain some of the riches that were to be found in the Americas.

France hired an Italian seaman named Verrazano. Early in 1542, he sailed along the coast of North America from Carolina to Nova Scotia. But he found no gold and no waterway to Asia.

Some ten years passed. By this time a Frenchman named Jacques Cartier was willing to seek the much-wanted route to the East. Cartier sailed up the St. Lawrence River as far as the site of Montreal but was unable to go further.

On another trip, he brought settlers and tried to settle a colony on the St. Lawrence. Many died. Discouragement and the lack of food, clothing, and shelter drove the remaining colonists home. Cartier's voyages gave France a claim to land in North America. But many years were to pass before permanent French settlements were made in what is now Canada and the Midwestern part of North America.

England Sends Explorers

Even before Columbus hired himself to Queen Isabella, another man born in Genoa named John Cabot tried several times to reach Asia by sailing west. Perhaps he didn't go far enough, or John Cabot would have discovered the Americas. Nevertheless, as soon as he heard of Columbus's success, Cabot talked again to some English merchants. They agreed that he should hurry and gain a share in the spice trade for them by sailing to the New World.

It took the English king three years to give his permission, but in 1497, Cabot and his son set off for the East in a small boat. They reached a large island covered with trees and claimed this "New Found Land" for England. They also discovered the fishing grounds of the Grand Banks—located southeast of Newfoundland, stretching 350 miles—that in later years brought great riches to the merchants of England.

Other trips by the Cabots did not convince the merchants that the Cabots had opened the way for trade, so they refused to hire them again. However, the merchants began sending fishermen to the Grand Banks for boatloads of fish. Years later, England claimed the Atlantic coast of North America because of the Cabots' voyages.

The English Sea Dogs

The English were not happy over the Cabots' failing to find a trade route through North America to Asia. They sent out other explorers, but all failed. As Spain got rich on stolen gold and Portugal built up a rich trade with the East, some English sea captains became pirates, or "seadogs." When they saw a Spanish ship headed home from the New World, they pulled down their British flag and put up the pirates' flag, the skull and crossbones. Then the English attacked. If successful, they took off the Indian treasure and sank the Spanish ship. The Spanish king made a big fuss about these pirates, but the English rulers said, "We can't stop piracy on the open seas. That will have to be your job."

Perhaps the most famous seadog was Sir Francis Drake. On one trip, Drake sailed down the coast of Africa. When he reached the equator, he crossed the Atlantic Ocean to the coast of South America. He sailed around South America into the Pacific Ocean. Here he surprised some Spanish ships and took their gold.

To escape from a Spanish warship, Drake sailed north. He traveled along the west coast of what is today the United States. Then he struck out boldly across the Pacific to sail around Africa and reach home. In this way, Drake sailed around the world. He brought back with him captured ships and large quantities of gold. Because of this, Queen Elizabeth knighted him.

The acts of the English seadogs were, in part, a form of retaliation against the acts of Spanish captains who often overtook English ships and forced English seamen to serve as slaves on Spanish ships. Nevertheless, the king of Spain would not tolerate any nation threatening his plans for world conquest.

The continual tension and acts of harassment between Spain and England ultimately lead these nations to the brink of war. Spain finally determined, once and for all, to crush the troublesome English who were keeping Spain from her dream of conquering the world and spreading the Roman Catholic religion. The king of Spain ordered his huge fleet of ships to sail against England, which was a Protestant nation. The Spanish sent their huge "Armada" of ships into the English Channel, confident of their ability to conquer England. The clumsy Spanish ships were attacked by a swarm of little English boats that managed to confuse the Spanish by their boldness. A short time later, in the providence of God, a great storm came upon the Armada. When the fog and wind finally let up, little remained of the once grand Spanish fleet. God had miraculously saved the English!

In the providence of God, a mighty storm arose and helped to defeat the Spanish Armada in one of the greatest sea battles in history.

In this way, Spain's sea power was broken in 1588. After that, England became a greater sea power. Her ships sailed far and wide, and eventually enabled England to gain a strong and dominant presence in North America.

One way or another, the nations of Europe tried to gain control of the Americas. This struggle among European nations, to establish colonies in the New World, lasted for many years. When you study the history of the United States, you will learn more about how the nations of England, France, Spain, and The Netherlands established colonies in North and South America during the sixteenth and seventeenth centuries. It should come as no surprise to students who have carefully considered this chapter why the nations of Europe were responsible for exploring and claiming much of the Americas. Students who understand the connection between the Old World nations of Europe and how they became involved in the Americas will have a solid basis on which to comprehend early American history.

CHAPTER SUMMARY

The nations of Europe wanted to build trade with the East. Because Venice and Genoa controlled the Mediterranean Sea, the other nations searched for a new way to reach China and India. In 1492, Columbus sailed west in hopes of reaching the East. He rediscovered the Americas.

Now that you have concluded your study of the Middle Ages, it should be clear why the people of Europe were responsible for exploring and developing the Americas. It should also be clear how many of the customs and religious beliefs from Old World Europe were eventually transplanted in North America.

England, France, Holland, and Spain sent explorers to the New World starting in the late fifteenth century through the early eighteenth century. Spaniards explored and claimed much of Central and South America, Mexico, and part of present-day United States. They also discovered the Pacific Ocean. Magellan's ships were the first to sail around the world and prove conclusively that the world was round.

Spain's Armada, once so great, was sunk in fifteen eighty-eight.

French explorers unsuccessfully sought to find a waterway to Asia but in the process were able to claim lands near and on the St. Lawrence River, the Mississippi River, and in parts of Canada. The Dutch explorers from Holland established a few early settlements in North America, the West Indies, and South America, although many of these settlements were eventually taken over by the British Empire.

It was England's explorers who found the Grand Banks fisheries and claimed the Atlantic Coast of North America. The work done by English explorers paved the way for the establishment of thirteen English colonies along the eastern coast of North America in the seventeenth and eighteenth centuries. Some English captains captured Spanish treasure ships in response to Spain's practice of kidnapping British seamen. The angry king of Spain attacked Protestant England and was beaten, when his "invincible" Armada was destroyed by a God-ordained storm at sea.

The defeat of the Spanish Armada put England in a dominant position to control most of the colonies in North America. For this reason, the American colonies were eventually settled primarily by Protestant English settlers rather than Roman Catholic settlers from Spain.

CHAPTER QUESTIONS AND ACTIVITIES

1. What was Prince Henry's dream?

2. Who was the first man to sail around Africa to India?

3. Name Columbus's three ships.

4. On what island did Columbus land?

5. Why was Columbus broken in spirit when he died in 1506?

6. About how long before 1492 did Leif Ericson visit North America?

7. What did Balboa discover?

8. Who claimed Florida for Spain?

9. Who was the first explorer to sail around the world?

10. How did Cortez get gold for Spain?

11. What country did Pizarro explore?

12. What kind of mines were developed in the Americas by Spain?

13. Who discovered the Mississippi River?

14. Coronado explored what part of North America?

15. Name two men who explored the New World for France.

16. Who were the English "seadogs"?

17. The Cabots explored what part of America?

18. Explain how Drake captured Spanish gold.

19. What was the Spanish Armada?

20. How was Spain's sea power broken?

21. Why did the nations of Europe want control of the New World?

22. Imagine you were with Magellan on the ship *Victoria*. Describe some of your experiences on this first trip around the world.

23. Try making a list of the products Europe wanted from the East.

KEY TERMS

Spyglass	Hispaniola
Navigation	Aztecs
Admiral	Armada

Index

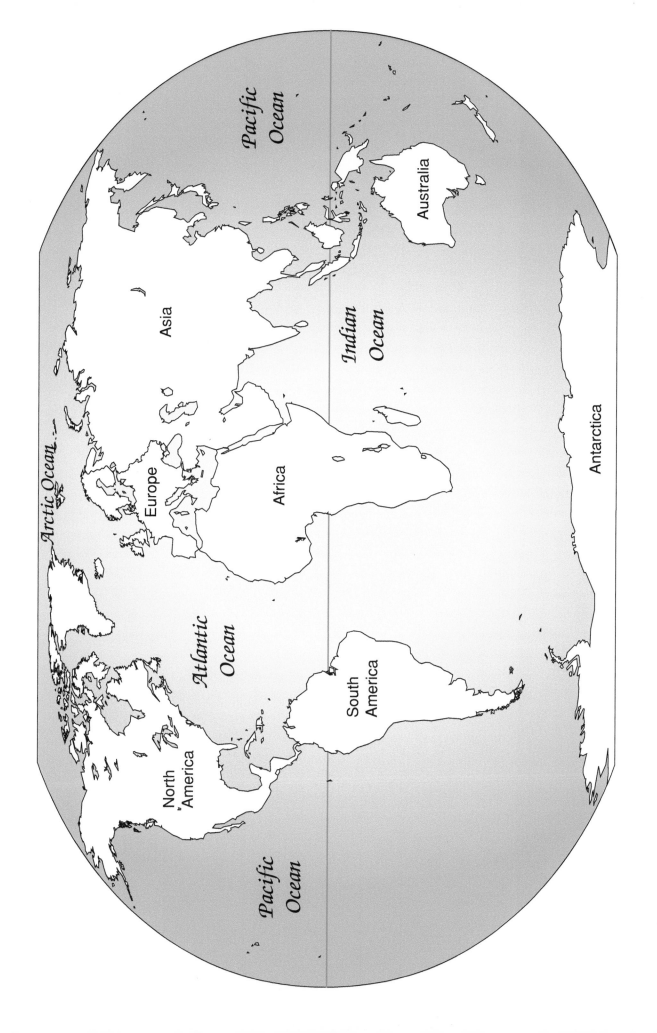

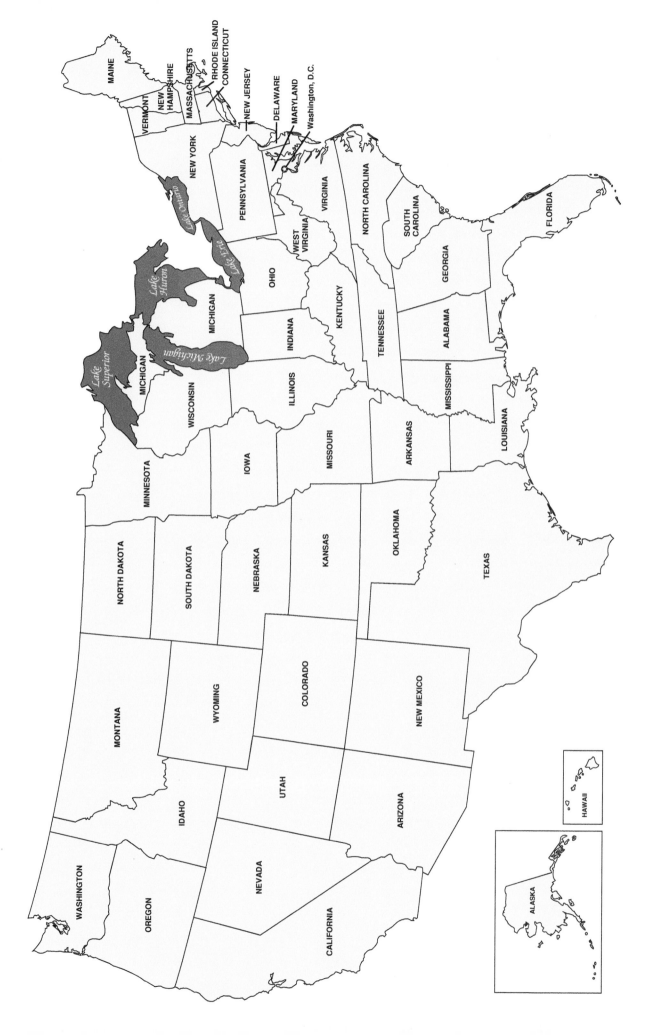